THE

HISTORY AND CONSTITUTION

OF THE

COURTS AND LEGISLATIVE AUTHORITIES IN INDIA

Owing to the antiquity and rarity of this book, certain pages are regrettably absent, and readability is compromised due to the blurring of the original text. If you possess any insights regarding the availability of these missing sections, kindly inform us. Your assistance is crucial in ensuring the completion of this significant work for the benefit of future generations.

THE

HISTORY AND CONSTITUTION

OF THE

COURTS AND LEGISLATIVE AUTHORITIES IN INDIA

BY

HERBERT COWELL

GYAN

Published by

GYAN

Gyan Publishing House
5, Ansari Road
Daryaganj, New Delhi-110002
Phone: 011-47034999, 9811692060
E-mail: books@gyanbooks.com

Distribution Network
gyanbooks.com
India, USA, Canada, UK, Australia

ISBN: 978-93-6433-520-1 (HB)
First Published, 1872

2nd Impression 2024

Printed at: Gyan Press, Delhi.

THE HISTORY AND CONSTITUTION OF THE COURTS AND LEGISLATIVE AUTHORITIES IN INDIA
Author: HERBERT COWELL

Tagore Law Lectures.

THE

HISTORY AND CONSTITUTION

OF THE

OURTS AND LEGISLATIVE AUTHORITIES IN INDIA.

BY

HERBERT COWELL, Esq.,

Barrister-at-Law, and Tagore Law Professor, 1869-1872.

Calcutta: THACKER, SPINK & CO.

London: W. THACKER & CO.

1905.

PREFACE.

THIS book concludes the labours of my three years' Professorship. It embraces a history of the Legislative Councils and of the judicial institutions which have been established in this country by the English; and an account is added of the existing Courts and Councils which make and administer the laws now in force in British India. The subject is one which is, in many respects, intricate and dull, but it is essential to an ordinary acquaintance with the Government and constitution of the empire.

H. C.

CALCUTTA, *August 12th*, 1872.

PREFACE TO THE FIFTH EDITION.

I HAVE retained the form of Lectures, as this book is mainly used by students. They speak as from 1905, and in Calcutta, instead of 1872, and are revised with reference to all enactments down to that date.

H. C.

2, HARCOURT BUILDINGS, TEMPLE, LONDON,
January 20, 1905.

TABLE OF CONTENTS.

LECTURE I.

EARLY HISTORY: THE GRANT OF THE DEWANNY.

LECTURE II.

EARLY HISTORY: THE REGULATING ACT.

LECTURE III.

EARLY HISTORY: THE SETTLEMENT OF 1781.

LECTURE IV.

THE LEGISLATIVE COUNCILS.

LECTURE V.

THE LEGISLATIVE COUNCILS—(*continued*).

LECTURE VI.

LATER HISTORY: THE PRESIDENCY TOWN SYSTEM.

LECTURE VII.

LATER HISTORY: THE PROVINCIAL CIVIL COURTS.

LECTURE X.

THE SUPERIOR COURTS.

LECTURE XI.

THE INFERIOR CIVIL COURTS.

LECTURE XII.

THE INFERIOR CRIMINAL COURTS AND POLICE.

LECTURE I.

EARLY HISTORY: THE GRANT OF THE DEWANNY.

Introduction—Commencement of established Institutions—Character of antecedent history—First introduction of Europeans into India—Early history of the East India Company—Territorial acquisitions—Fall of the Mogul Empire—Aggressive policy of the Company—Settlement in Bengal—Position of the English before their Conquest—Legislative Authority of the Company during that period—Charter of Elizabeth—Of James I.—Of Charles II.—Of William III.—Charters of 1726 and 1753—Judicial Authority of the Company during that period—Necessity for obtaining it—Early Charters—Mayors' Courts—Jurisdiction of the Governor and Council—Mayors' Courts and Courts of Requests—Subjugation of Bengal—Civil Disorders and Anarchy—Elements of Civil Order—Relations of the Mogul, the Nabob, the Crown and the Company—First Attempt to re-organize Society—Grant of the Dewanny—Its effect—No Judicial Coercion over Europeans—Reforms of Lord Clive—Necessity for Grant of Definite Authority.

I SHALL endeavour to present in this course of lectures a general view of the legislative power and judicial authority now and heretofore exercised in British India. And in doing so it is unnecessary to refer with the accustomed detail to the various enactments passed during the rule of the Company in reference to this subject. The earlier legislation is treated at length in Harrington's Analysis, which was published in 1805; and a long string of Acts and Regulations is to be found in Auber's Analysis, Morley's Digest, and other works. But my object in this volume is to separate the existing legislative and judicial institutions from the previous history of those

Introduction.

Lecture I.

institutions, reducing the latter as much as possible to a continuous narrative. The subject is preliminary to the study of the laws in force in British India, and deals with the character and powers of the councils and tribunals which respectively make and administer those laws. In any question of difficulty as to the source and early boundaries of power in reference to any institution, the particular enactments relating to it must always be consulted. So far as regards the legislation of the past, its general character and historical bearing will here alone be explained; that which regulates existing institutions will be treated in greater detail.

The suppression of the Indian Mutinies and the assumption of the government in name as well as in reality by the English Crown led to a consolidation and re-establishment of the Indian Empire; and the year 1861, in which the Indian Councils' Act and the Indian High Courts' Act were passed, marks the close of a tedious and intricate period of Indian constitutional history. Those enactments and the subsequent legislation which has been effected here, especially during the legal membership of Mr. FitzJames Stephen, are the foundation of nearly the whole judicial and legislative authorities now existing in India. I may therefore say at the outset that at that date I shall divide the historical sketch of the earlier institutions from the account of the existing constitution of the Courts and Legislative authorities here established. The time has come when most of the legislation on these subjects, even down to the very recent period which I have mentioned, is no longer of detailed interest requiring constant reference. It has passed into the region of history as completely as the victories of Clive and the policy of Hastings; and in order to be of the slightest interest, must be studied in reference to the political circumstances which influenced it and the conflicting interests and passions which lay behind it.

Lecture I.

Constitutional history in this country has nothing to do with the steady spontaneous growth of national institutions. It is a record of experiments made by foreign rulers to govern alien races in a strange land, to adapt European institutions to Oriental habits of life, and to make definite laws supreme amongst peoples who had always associated government with arbitrary and uncontrolled authority. There is considerable vacillation of purpose exhibited in those experiments, influenced as they were by conflicts of opinion and the rivalry of interests, but on the whole there was a steady advance towards securing impartial justice and legislation.

Commencement of established institutions.

The year 1781 marks the most important era in the history now under consideration. It terminated a period of fierce animosity and struggle between those who wished to see English law and Courts of Justice introduced at once into the country and rendered supreme over the Executive, and those who considered that such a policy was wholly impracticable, and that, circumstanced as the English then were, Government must for a long time to come control the authority of the Courts. It commenced the era of independent Indian legislation; of the authority of the Supreme Court, as it continued more or less to be exercised for eighty years; of the establishment of a Board of Revenue "entrusted with the charge and administration of all the public revenues of the provinces, and invested in the fullest manner with all powers and authority, under the control of the Governor-General and Council;" * of the recognition by Act of Parliament of the established Sudder and Provincial Courts; and of the recognition by Act of Parliament and in the Revised Code of Bengal of the right of Hindus and Mahomedans to be governed by their own laws and usages. The plan of government, both as regards legislation and the Courts of Justice, in that year assumed a definite shape, and although

* 2 Harrington's Analysis, p. 35.

LECTURE I.

many changes of course ensued in the long period (1781—1861) which separated the administration of Warren Hastings, the first Governor-General of India, from the close of that of Lord Canning, its first Viceroy, still they were changes of detail, often of great importance, but leaving unaltered the general character of the system then introduced.

Confining ourselves therefore in the first place to the exclusively historical portion of the subject, I shall take the year 1781 as the dividing point of time at which the character of that history essentially changes, at which the boundaries of authority have at last become strongly defined.

Character of antecedent history.

Previous to that date the general character of Indian history, or of the history of the government by the English of their Indian possessions, is one of military struggle and civil tumult interspersed with occasional efforts to organize society. A vivid description of it is given by Lord Macaulay in his celebrated Essays on Lord Clive and Warren Hastings. The chief centres of interest are the individual efforts and achievements of the two powerful chiefs who laid the foundation of the British Empire in India, and to whom the natives of India owe a juster government, greater security, greater wealth, and means of social happiness and order than they ever experienced before or would ever have been likely to obtain had Clive and Hastings never lived.

Previous to that date, moreover, as it seems to me, the history of Courts and Legislatures is mingled with the history of the Executive, and they must be pursued together. For notwithstanding the desperate attempt in 1773, by means of the Supreme Court then established, to introduce law and order, the rash and ignorant though well-intentioned policy of which that scheme betrays the existence only increased the civil confusion, and in the midst of the greatest disorder almost paralyzed the authority of government, without substituting any other means of security for life and property.

It will be convenient, therefore, to divide the history of this subject into two portions; to give a general view of the Company, its conquests and its efforts at social organization with reference to surrounding circumstances down to 1781, and afterwards to trace separately the subsequent history of the legislative and judicial institutions, which by that time had sprung into separate and definite existence.

The first branch of the subject is worthy of considerable attention. It includes within its scope the two most important events of the grant of the Dewanny by the Mogul Emperor, and the Parliamentary attempt to settle Indian affairs by the Regulating Act. Those occurrences refer exclusively to Bengal. The other Presidencies were governed in imitation of the policy pursued by the Supreme Government in reference to the chief Presidency. The problems of difficulty were worked out in Bengal and their solution was transferred to Madras and Bombay.

First introduction of Europeans into India.

To start from the beginning, I may remind you that the Portuguese were the first European nation who persevered in carrying on trade and acquiring dominion in India. Their countryman Vasco di Gama had discovered the passage round the Cape of Good Hope, and thus for a whole century conferred upon the nation to which he belonged a monopoly of trade and commerce in the East. Subsequently the Dutch followed the Portuguese, and subverted their power. Finally English merchants endeavoured to prosecute trade with India, and their efforts proving successful, a Charter was granted by Queen Elizabeth in the year 1600, incorporating the London East India Company, and giving to them the exclusive right of trading to all parts of Asia, Africa, and America beyond the Cape of Good Hope, eastward to the Straits of Magellan.

Early history of the East India Company.

With regard to the existence of the Company, it seems that after the restoration of Charles II. various attacks were

LECTURE I.

made upon the existence and enjoyment of exclusive rights which had been conferred by the Crown irrespective of Parliament; but they were made without effect. In 1698,* however, another Company was incorporated under authority of an Act of Parliament by a separate Charter under the name of the English East India Company. Ten years afterwards the two Companies were united under the award of Lord Godolphin in the sixth year of Queen Anne; the Charter granted by William III. in 1698 remaining as the foundation of the privileges of the united Company, under which the Court of Directors was constituted and the General Court of Proprietors was vested with the chief authority and control over the affairs of the Company. This constitution remained unchanged till the Regulating Act of 1773, under the provisions of which statute a Governor-General and Council were first nominated, with power over the whole of the Company's possessions in India, a Board of Control being shortly afterwards formed at home.

During the sixty-five years which elapsed from the union of the two Companies under the award of Lord Godolphin down to the Regulating Act of 1773, great acquisitions of territory were made; and the position of the Company was gradually changed from that of tenants of factories, owing obedience to the Mogul Emperor, to one of practical and independent sovereignty.

Territorial acquisitions.

With regard to acquisitions of territory, the first possession of the English was the island of Bombay, ceded to Charles II. in 1661 by the King of Portugal as part of the marriage dowry of the Infanta. Charles II. granted it to the East India Company, which about the same time gained possession of some factories on the west coast of India. Somewhat later, factories were established at Madras and other places on the east coast. Last of all the Company made

* See 9 & 10 William & Mary, Chap. 44.

trading settlements in Bengal, and founded Calcutta. The factories of Bombay, Madras, and Calcutta became the leading factories in their different localities, and exercised control and supervision over the subordinate depôts and places in their vicinity.

Fall of the Mogul Empire.

The ruin of the Mogul Empire proceeded with great rapidity after the death of Aurungzeb in 1707. He was succeeded by a series of nominal sovereigns, whose dominions were invaded and whose authority was defied. The Mahrattas overran the country, which they either subjected to their rule or wasted by their plunder Even the European factories were in danger, and the settlement of Calcutta was fortified and enclosed within the Mahratta ditch. It was during this feud between the Mahratta and the Mahomedan, which spread from one end of the empire to the other, and threw the whole peninsula into confusion, that the French and English first began the work of conquest and annexation. The conquests of the French, the principal of which were in the Madras Presidency, were first disputed by Clive in the year 1750, and from that time the power of the English continued steadily to increase, and that of the French to decline. In a very few years the English occupation of Madras was placed beyond the reach of French aggression; the vigour and force which the long rivalry had developed serving for the time to secure to the Presidency of Madras the leading rank in the Company's settlements

Aggressive policy of the Company.

Thus Madras became the most important possession of the Company. It was the scene of the early victories of Lord Clive, and of the first successful efforts to acquire political power and dominion over the country. It was not, however, till the middle of the 18th century that the Company began to combine military and political aims with the ordinary pursuits of a mercantile corporation. Its rivalry with the French, the neighbourhood of the Mahrattas, and the frequent attacks to which it was in consequence exposed speedily converted its Madras servants into soldiers, and paved the way to occasional conquests. Eventually the decay of the Mahomedan power in India, the incursions of the Mahrattas, and the rivalry of the French rendered it necessary for the Company to choose between immediate withdrawal and a policy of aggression.

Settlement in Bengal.

Up to this time, although the English had built Fort William and settled in Bengal, they had not departed from the character of merchants and factors. The accession of Surajah Dowlah in 1756, who entered upon a policy of repression which he had not the resources to sustain, was the commencement of a series of struggles which ended in the establishment of the Company's authority in the Lower and afterwards in the Upper Provinces of Bengal. The capture of Fort William and the tragedy of the Black Hole roused the vengeance of the settlement at Madras. Clive came to Bengal, recovered Calcutta, and in the next year (1757), by the battle of Plassey, destroyed the power of Surajah Dowlah, and obtained possession of Moorshedabad, with authority over the whole of Bengal.

Position of the English before their conquest.

The foregoing observations will serve as a sketch of the origin and progress of the Company and its conquests down to and shortly after the battle of Plassey. During this period wherever the English settled, except in the island of Bombay, which had been ceded in full sovereignty to Charles II., the general character of their position was that it was obtained by leave of the Native Government. In Bengal especially their settlements were founded and their factories fortified with that leave, in districts purchased from the owners of the soil by permission of that Government, and held under it by the Company as subjects owing obedience, as tenants rendering rent, and even as officers exercising by delegation a part of the authority of the Native Government.*

The ordinary consequences of this state of things would have been to render the English subject to the Native Government and amenable to its laws. They could not, however, be governed by the law of the Koran, and therefore from necessity they remained subject to their own law, and were obliged to take measures for introducing and administering it. Before the English assumed sovereign powers and independence of native authority, their position was extremely anomalous. Though their factories were part of the dominion of the Mogul, their own law was administered in them, and their own national character imparted to them as completely as if they were parts of English territory. A foreigner residing in them and carrying on trade was held to take his temporary national character not from the Mogul dominion, to which they were subject, but from the British possessions.†

Legislative authority of the Company during that period.

Under these circumstances, it became necessary in very early days of the existence of the Company that the Crown should grant to them certain legislative and judicial authority to be exercised in their East Indian possessions. That authority, however, it seems clear, was only intended to be exercised over their English servants and such native settlers as placed themselves under their protection. With regard to the early legislative authority, the Charter of Queen Elizabeth in 1601 granted to the Governor and Company or the more part of them being assembled power, long before they possessed any territory or sovereign authority, "to make, ordain, and constitute such and so many reasonable laws, constitutions, orders, and ordinances, as to them or the greater part

Charter of Elizabeth.

* See judgment of Lord Brougham in the *Mayor of Lyons* v. *East India Company*, 1 Moore's Indian Appeals, p. 272.

† See the *Indian Chief*, per Lord Stowell, 3 Rob. Adm. Rep., p. 29.

LECTURE I.

of them being then and there present, shall seem necessary and convenient for the good government of the said Company and of all factors, masters, mariners, and other officers employed or to be employed in any of their voyages, and for the better advancement and continuance of their trade and traffic." They were also empowered to put in use and execute such laws, "and at their pleasure to revoke and alter the same or any of them as occasion shall require," and to provide such pains and penalties by imprisonment or fine as might seem to them necessary to secure their due observance.

of James I.

James I. by his Charter, granted in 1609, renewed the same power, both Charters containing the proviso "so always as the said laws, orders, constitutions, ordinances, imprisonments, fines, and amerciaments be reasonable and not contrary or repugnant to the laws, statutes, or customs of this our realm."

of Charles II.

Charles II.'s Charter, granted in 1661, contained a similar provision.

In the Charter relating to the island of Bombay, of which the sovereignty had been ceded, granted by Charles II. in the year 1669, a similar power of legislation was given.

All these early Charters were surrendered when the two Companies were amalgamated under the award of Lord Godolphin. The laws passed in pursuance of them were directed to be published; but no trace of them now exists. They probably were for the most part concerned with the trade of the Company, preserving its monopoly and repressing interference. It is probable that the powers were not extensively used, but it was necessary that they should exist, in order to provide for any emergency that might arise.

of William III.

The Charter granted by William III. in 1698 became the foundation of the United Company, which was subsequently called the East India Company.* By it, the Company were

* *Vide* 3 & 4 Wm. IV., Chap. 85, Section 111.

vested with the government of all their forts, factories, and plantations, the sovereign power being reserved for the Crown. Courts of Judicature were also established as before, but nothing was then said about a power of legislation.

LECTURE I.

In George I.'s Charter of 1726, which also established the Mayors' Courts, the Governors and Councils of the three Presidencies were vested with the power "to make, constitute, and ordain bye-laws, rules, and ordinances for the good government and regulation of the several corporations hereby created, and of the inhabitants of the several towns, places, and factories aforesaid respectively, and to impose reasonable pains and penalties upon all persons offending against the same or any of them." Such laws and penalties were to be agreeable to reason, and not contrary to the laws and statutes of England. They were not to have any force or effect until the same had been approved and confirmed by order in writing of the Court of Directors. And then the Charter proceeded: "We do hereby ordain and declare that none of the corporations hereby created shall have a power or authority to make any bye-laws, rules, or ordinances whatsoever other than such rules as they are respectively by these presents empowered to make." The Charter of 1753 gave a similar power, omitting the passage quoted.

Charters of 1726 and 1753.

With regard to the grant of judicial authority to be exercised in the Company's settlements, we might reasonably expect that it would be called for and required before the necessity arose for establishing any legislative authority. The actual decision of disputes in an infant society is of practical importance long before the necessity of a definite body of rules is felt. Moreover, the English were supposed to bring with them such of their own laws as were applicable to them in the circumstances in which they were placed. And factories established amongst races alien in religion, habits and customs have always been deemed by the law of

Judicial authority of the Company during that period.

LECTURE I.

nations which has prevailed in Christendom to be so far exclusive possessions, or at least privileged places, that all persons during their residence within them have been considered for most purposes to be clothed with the national character of the State to which the factory has belonged.

Necessity for obtaining it.

Accordingly it seems that as early as 1618, Sir Thomas Roe, the Ambassador of James I., had secured by treaty with the Mogul the privilege for the factory at Surat, that disputes between the English only should be decided by themselves. The East India Company, before the end of the 17th century, had obtained and made use of permission to build fortifications at Madras and Calcutta, and thus established and defended their own authority within their own factories. Under these fortifications, Natives built houses as well as Europeans. And when the Nawab* on that account was about to send a Kaji, or Judge, to administer justice to the Natives, the Company's servants bribed him to abstain from this proceeding. At the same time they held the island of Bombay under a grant in perpetuity from the Crown of England. It was absolutely essential, therefore, in very early days that some authority to administer justice and some regularly constituted judicial authorities should exist in the possessions of the Company.

Early Charters.

In the earliest Charters granted by the Crown, power was given to the Company in a general and indistinct way to administer justice to those who should live under them. In 1661 Charles II. gave by Royal Charter to the Governor and Council of the several places belonging to the Company in the East Indies power "to judge all persons belonging to the said Governor and Company or that should live under them in all causes, whether civil or criminal, according to the laws of the kingdom, and to execute justice accordingly." In

* See judgment of Lord Brougham in *Mayor of Lyons* v. *East India Company*, 1 Moore's Indian Appeals, p. 272.

grants to the Company within the next thirteen years of the islands of Bombay and St. Helena, full power was given for the exercise by the Company of Judicial authority according to the British laws. And in 1683 Charles II. granted a further Charter in which the royal will was declared that a Court of Judicature should be established at such places as the Company might appoint; to consist of one person learned in the Civil laws and two merchants all to be appointed by the Company and to decide according to equity and good conscience and according to the laws and customs of merchants by such rules as the Crown should from time to time direct either by the Great Seal or Privy Seal; failing which directions by such ways and means as the Judges should think best. These provisions were continued in some subsequent Charters, but they do not appear to have been effectual for the purpose for which they were framed.

Mayors' Courts.

In less than twenty years after the United Company was established under the Act of Queen Anne, its Court and Directors represented by petition to George I. that there was great want at Madras, Fort William, and Bombay of a proper and competent power and authority for the more speedy and effectual administering of justice in civil causes, and for trying and punishing of capital and other criminal offences and misdemeanours; and they accordingly prayed permission to establish Mayors' Courts at these places. Thereupon the existing Courts, whatever they may have been, were superseded, and in the year 1726 (13th Geo. I.) the Crown by Letters Patent established Mayors' Courts at Madras, Bombay, and Fort William, each consisting of a Mayor and nine Aldermen, seven of whom with the Mayor were required to be natural born British subjects. They were declared to be Courts of Record, and were empowered to try, hear, and determine all civil suits, actions, and pleas between party and party.

Lecture I.

Jurisdiction of the Governor and Council.

By virtue of the same Letters Patent each Local Government consisting of a Governor and Council was constituted a Government Court of Record to which appeals from the decision of the Mayor's Court might be made. In causes involving sums under 1000 pagodas,* the decision of the Government Court was final; if the sum involved was above that amount an appeal lay from the Government Court to the King in Council. The Government Court was further constituted a Court of Oyer and Terminer, and was authorized and required to hold Quarter Sessions for the trial of all offences excepting high treason. The Mayors' Courts were empowered to grant probates of wills and administration to the effects of intestates.

The Charter of George I. recited that the Company "had by a strict and equal distribution of justice very much encouraged not only our own subjects, but likewise the subjects of other princes and the natives of adjacent countries to resort to and settle in the said forts, towns, factories, and places, by which means some of them had become very populous, especially the places called Madras, Bombay, and Fort William in Bengal." It also recited that "there was great want in all the said places and in other settlements of the Company of a proper and competent power and authority for the more speedy and effectual administering of justice in civil causes and for the trying and punishing of capital and other criminal offences and misdemeanours." The criminal trials were directed to be conducted "in the same or the like manner and form as near as the conditions and circumstances of the place and inhabitants will admit of as any our Justices of the Peace or Commissioners of Oyer and Terminer and Gaol Delivery do or may proceed by virtue of any commission by us granted for that purpose."

* A pagoda is a Madras coin, never current in Bengal, of the value of about eight shillings of English money.

Mayors' Courts and Courts of Requests.

This Charter was superseded by the Charter granted to the same Company in 1753 (26 Geo. II.), which re-established Mayors' Courts at Madras, Bombay, and Calcutta, with some amendments intended to remedy defects of which the Company had complained. The new Letters Patent also established a Court of Requests at each of the said places for the determination of suits "where the debt duty or matter in dispute should not exceed five pagodas." Both Courts were made subject to a control on the part of the Court of Directors, who were authorised by the Letters Patent to make "bye-laws, rules, and ordinances for the good government and regulation of the several Courts of Judicature established in India." The chief alteration effected by the new Letters Patent was that the Courts which they established were limited in their civil jurisdiction to suits between persons who were not Natives of the several towns to which the jurisdiction applied. Suits between Natives were directed not to be entertained by the Mayors' Courts unless by consent of the parties.

These Letters continued in force in Bengal for about twenty years, and in Madras and Bombay for a longer period. A committee of secrecy, appointed to enquire into the state of the East India Company, observed with reference to the Mayors' Courts that the Judges were justly sensible of their own deficiency and had frequently applied to the Court of Directors for assistance. Application was thereupon made to the Crown for a new Charter of Justice for Bengal.

Thus the first Courts of Record established in Bengal existed for nearly fifty years. It does not appear whether in the original Letters Patent or in those which with some alterations were substituted for them in 1753, there was any intention on the part of the Crown to assert any territorial dominion. In the Charter of 1753, although there was no precedent for it in the Charter of 1726, civil suits between

Lecture I.

Natives were expressly excepted from the jurisdiction of the Mayors' Courts, and directed to be determined among themselves; which appears to involve a renunciation of sovereign authority at that time over Natives.

Subjugation of Bengal.

This, then, was the extent of legislative and judicial authority possessed by the Company at the time when the events which succeeded the battle of Plassey (A.D. 1757) compelled them to undertake the task of reconstituting and reorganizing society in the Lower Provinces of Bengal, *i.e.* to assume all the functions of sovereignty. A period of greater political confusion than that which followed the subjugation of those provinces it is impossible to imagine. The conquered were without spirit or means of defence; the conquerors exhibited all that ravening for plunder which sudden and easy acquisition of wealth inspires, possessed scarcely any of the elements of social union themselves, and were both unwilling and unable to undertake the duties of government. The position was pregnant with all the evils which the Normans introduced amongst the conquered Saxons in England, evils of rapine, plunder, and tyranny, without the redeeming accompaniments of the strong government and determined spirit of order which belonged to the Norman conquerors, who were the most civilised people of early Europe, and the most advanced in the arts of government and in political organization. The victors of Bengal were for the most part anxious to plunder, and then withdraw from a climate which they regarded as fatal; they were separated by a year's journey from the government to which they owed allegiance, and were as a general rule incapable, from their habits and knowledge and previous pursuits, of conceiving higher aspirations or duties than those of augmenting the dividends of their Company.

Civil disorders and anarchy.

Shortly after the subjugation of Bengal, Clive departed to England, and during the five years which followed, the

misgovernment of the English, says Lord Macaulay, was carried to a point such as seems hardly compatible with the very existence of society. They pulled down one prince and set up another in his turn, and on each accession to the throne, the new monarch divided among his foreign masters the treasures of his predecessor. The position of the Natives under these circumstances is vigorously described by Lord Macaulay :—" The servants of the Company obtained not for their employers, but for themselves a monopoly of almost the whole internal trade.* They forced the Natives to buy dear and to sell cheap. They insulted with impunity the tribunals, the police and the fiscal authorities of the country. They covered with their protection a set of Native dependents who ranged through the provinces spreading desolation and terror wherever they appeared. Every servant of a British factor was armed with all the power of his master ; and his master was armed with all the power of the Company. Enormous fortunes were thus rapidly accumulated at Calcutta, while thirty millions of human beings were reduced to the extremity of wretchedness. They had been accustomed to live under tyranny, but never under tyranny like this. They found the little finger of the Company thicker than the loins of Surajah Dowlah. Under their old masters they had at least one resource : when the evil became insupportable, the people rose and pulled down the Government. But the English government was not to be so shaken off. That government, oppressive as the most oppressive form of barbarian despotism, was strong with all the strength of civilization. It resembled the government of evil genii rather than the government of human tyrants. * * * * *
The unhappy race never attempted resistance. Sometimes they submitted in patient misery, sometimes they fled from the white man as their fathers had been used to fly from the

* Macaulay's Essays, Vol. III., p. 177.

LECTURE I.

Mahratta; and the palanquin of the English traveller was often carried through silent villages and towns which the report of his approach had made desolate."

Elements of civil order.

The position was shortly this. The servants of a mercantile company, with some judicial and legislative authority existing amongst them wholly inadequate even to their own requirements, with all bands of discipline totally relaxed, were the military masters of the country, practically freed from all control from England. Sovereignty and the right of administering civil and criminal justice were vested in the Mogul Emperor, whose government of the provinces of Bengal consisted * of two parts: the Dewanny or collection of the revenues and the administration of the principal branches of the department of civil justice, and the Nizamut or the military branch of the government, with the superintendence of the criminal department of judicature: and of these the Dewanny was subordinate to the Nizamut.

Relations of the Mogul, the Nabob, the Crown and the Company.

The powers and duties of the native government had long been delegated to the Nabob of Moorshedabad, but the victories of the English had finally dislodged his authority. Those victories in reality transferred the rights of sovereignty to the English Crown; but the seat of that Government was in London, and it was practically impossible for the Crown to exercise its rights. The Company, on the other hand, were by no means desirous of invoking the aid of the Government at home; they regarded any step in that direction as one which tended to introduce a power into India which was likely to prove fatal to their revenues and authority. The Directors of the Company prescribed mercy and justice, but demanded an enormous revenue, which it was impossible to obtain without oppression and wrong. No restraint of moral duty or legal responsibility deterred the conquerors, while the only authority in England which they recognized, *viz.*, the Court of

* Mill's History of India, Vol. IV., p. 19.

Directors, virtually and practically encouraged the excesses of their administration. Scenes of misery and oppression ensued which Lord Macaulay stigmatises as the most frightful which the world has seen, a prostrate people exposed to all the strength of civilization without its mercy.

LECTURE I.

First attempt to reorganize society.

Lord Clive, in 1765, landed in India for the third time to undertake duties as considerable and as arduous as those which devolved on William the Conqueror after the battle of Hastings. The independence of the natives was crushed, while the means at his disposal for the organization of government were of the slenderest description. He decided at once to avail himself of the outstanding sovereignty of the Mogul. The Directors of the Company stood between him and the sovereignty of the English Crown; and that source of authority, the most obvious one to resort to, was consequently denied to him. He proceeded to obtain the grant of the Dewanny from the Mogul Emperor.

Grant of the Dewanny.

That act is generally regarded as the acquisition of sovereignty by the English. The collection of revenue in India involved the whole administration of civil justice, and that, together with actual possession and military power, nearly completed the full idea of sovereignty. Still in name it was held in vassalage from the Mogul; and the Nizamut or administration of criminal justice remained with the Mogul's lieutenant, the Nabob of Moorshedabad.

Although the grant of the Dewanny is generally regarded as the grant of sovereignty for the want of any better and more formal transference of power, yet its real motive and intention were to avoid that acquisition. It, however, vested in the Company's government the reality or the semblance of legitimate authority over the natives, which, together with the actual military power, was sufficient for the purposes of government. The view which the Directors took of the transaction is as follows:—

LECTURE I.

"We conceive * the office of Dewan should be exercised only in superintending the collection and disposal of the revenues. This we conceive to be the whole office of the Dewan. The administration of justice, the appointments to offices, zemindaries, in short, whatever comes under the denomination of civil administration, we understand, is to remain in the hands of the Nawab or his ministers."

Its effect.

So far, however, as authority over the English servants of the Company were concerned, whom it was Lord Clive's object firmly to restrain, the difficulties were as great as ever. His power to inflict upon them adequate punishment either for disobedience to orders or for any other species of misconduct was in a civil point of view limited to the slender powers conferred on the Mayors' Courts. Neither he nor the Directors could derive from the Mogul Emperor authority over Englishmen or Europeans. The only authority then existing in India to which they were amenable was derived from the Charter of Justice which established the Mayors' Courts in 1753. That Charter renewed the Courts of 1726, which were established in the infancy of British rule, with a view to maintain order in a few factories, and were totally inadequate to the wants of government after the battle of Plassey and the conquest of Bengal.

For, so far as Bengal was concerned, it simply empowered the Mayor's Court of Calcutta, as a Court of Record, to try all civil suits arising between Europeans within the town or factory of Calcutta, or the factories dependent upon it; it also constituted the President and Council a Court of Record, to receive and determine appeals from the Mayors; it further erected them into Justices of the Peace with power to hold quarter sessions; and into Commissioners of Oyer and Terminer, and general gaol-delivery for the trying and punishing of all offences, high treason excepted,

* Despatch of 17th May, 1768, and see Torrens' Empire in Asia, p. 63.

committed within the limits of Calcutta and its dependent factories.

Lecture I.

No judicial coercion over Europeans.

This extent of jurisdiction, says Mr. Mill,* measured by the sphere of the Company's possessions at the time when it was granted, withheld all powers of judicial coercion with regard to Europeans over the wide extent of territory of which they now acted as the sovereigns. The Company possessed indeed the power of suing or prosecuting Englishmen in the Courts of Westminster; but under the necessity of bringing evidence from India, this was a privilege more nominal than real. And in case of an Indian Governor or Judge exceeding the scanty and inadequate power which he possessed, he was liable in an action in the same Courts.

Reforms of Lord Clive.

It is fairly claimed in praise of Lord Clive that, during the twenty months in which he ruled Bengal, he effected considerable reforms. The chief was the prohibition of the private trade of the servants of the Company, and the substitution of a liberal system of remuneration. By these means the rapid acquisition of wealth was stopped, and one great motive for oppression and extortion was removed. He also, by obtaining the grant of the Dewanny, placed the government of Bengal on a legal basis, and established its relations to the natives on a footing of definite civil responsibility.

Necessity for grant of definite authority.

"The power of the English in that province," says Lord Macaulay,† "had hitherto been altogether undefined. It was unknown to the ancient constitution of the empire, and it had been ascertained by no compact. It resembled the power which, in the last decrepitude of the Western Empire, was exercised over Italy by the great chiefs of foreign mercenaries, the Ricimers and the Odoacers, who put up and pulled down at their pleasure a succession of insignificant

* Mill's History of India, Vol. III., p. 343.

† Macaulay's Essays, Vol. III., p. 186.

LECTURE I.

princes, dignified with the names of Cæsar and Augustus. But as in Italy, so in India, the warlike strangers at length found it expedient to give to a domination which had been established by arms the sanction of law and ancient prescription. Theodore thought it politic to obtain from the distant Court of Byzantium a commission appointing him ruler of Italy; and Clive in the same manner applied to the Court of Delhi for a formal grant of the powers of which he already possessed the reality. The Mogul was absolutely helpless; and, though he murmured, had reason to be well pleased that the English were disposed to give solid rupees which he never could have extorted from them in exchange for a few Persian characters which cost him nothing. A bargain was speedily struck; and the titular sovereign of Hindoostan issued a warrant empowering the Company to collect and administer the revenues of Bengal, Orissa, and Behar."

NOTE:—I subjoin * the text of the Firmaund granted by the King Shah Alum to the Company in 1765.

At this happy time our royal Firmaund, indispensably requiring obedience, is issued; that, whereas, in consideration of the attachment and services of the high and mighty, the noblest of exalted nobles, the chief of illustrious warriors, our faithful servants and sincere well-wishers, worthy of our royal favours, the English Company, we have granted them the Dewanny of the Provinces of Bengal, Behar, and Orissa, from the beginning of the Fussel Rubby of the Bengal year 1172, as a free gift and ultumgan, without the association of any other person, and with an exemption of the payment of the customs of the Dewanny, which used to be paid by the Court. It is requisite that the said Company engage to be security for the sum of 26 lakhs of rupees a year for our royal revenue, which sum has been appointed from the Nabob Nudjum-ul-Dowla Behauder, and regularly remit the same to the royal Circar; and in this case, as the said Company are obliged to keep up a large Army for the Protection of the Provinces of Bengal, &c., we have granted to them whatsoever may remain out of the revenues of the said provinces, after remitting the sum of 26 lakhs of rupees to the royal Circar, and providing for the expenses of the Nizamut. It is

* Aitchison's Treaties (India), p. 60.

requisite that our royal descendants, the Viziers, the bestowers of dignity, the Omrahs high in rank, the great officers, the Muttaseddees of the Dewanny, the manager of the business of the Sultanut, the Jaghirdars and Croories, as well the future as the present using their constant endeavours for the establishment of this our royal command, leave the said office in possession of the said Company, from generation to generation for ever and ever. Looking upon them to be assured from dismissal or removal, they must, on no account whatsoever, give them any interruption, and they must regard them as excused and exempted from the payment of all the customs of the Dewanny and royal demands. Knowing our orders on the subject to be most strict and positive, let them not deviate therefrom.—*Written the 24th of Sophar, of the 6th year of the Jaloos, the 12th of August*, 1765.

LECTURE II.

EARLY HISTORY: THE REGULATING ACT.

Grant of the Dewanny—Its Consequences—Antecedent Position of the Native Courts—Native Agency in Civil Justice retained till 1772 under Supervision—The Company's Supervision thereof—Authority of Native Dewans—Supervision gradually extended—Native Agency in Criminal Justice retained—Change of Policy—The Company undertake the Administration of Civil Justice—Also of Criminal Justice—Chief Criminal Court—Chief Civil Court—Character of Warren Hastings' Plan of 1772—Interference of English Government and Public Opinion—Policy of the Directors—Policy of Parliament—The Regulating Act—Provisions for Executive Government—For Legislation—For Establishment of Supreme Court—The Charter—Its Jurisdiction as a Common Law Court—As an Equity Court—As a Criminal Court—As an Ecclesiastical Court—As an Admiralty Court—Appeals from the Court to the Privy Council—Indefinite Terms of the Act and Charter—Relation of the Court to the Council—Powers of the Court, and conduct of the Judges—The Result—Failure of the Court.

Grant of the Dewanny.

THE grant of the Dewanny was accompanied by an imperial confirmation of all the territories previously held by the East India Company under grants from the Emperor. The Nizamut or administration of criminal justice was left in the hands of the Nabob, who received for its support and his own maintenance an annual grant of 53 lakhs of rupees. He thus recognised his dependence, and although the Nizamut remained in his hands, it was, or at any time might be exercised under the control of the Company.

Its consequences.

The Company thus became responsible for the collection of the revenue, and directly or indirectly for the due administration of civil and criminal justice. Nevertheless, for a period of six years, the latter duty was as a heavy and unproductive burden left in the hands of the Nabob; the criminal part belonging to the Nazim or military governor; the civil, to the Dewan or fiscal governor.* The result was that for a time the course of justice was suspended, the tribunals being without authority against the masters of the country.

Antecedent position of the native Courts.

And "under the ancient Government,"† says Mr. Mill, "the English, as well as other European settlers, instead of demanding payment from a reluctant debtor through the Courts of law, seized his person and confined it till satisfaction was obtained. Nor was this so inconsistent with the spirit of the Government as often to excite its displeasure. It was indeed a remedy to which they were not often obliged to recur, because the profit of dealing with them generally constituted a sufficient motive to punctuality. After the power of the English became predominant, the native Courts ceased to exert any authority over Englishmen and their agents." The loss of all title to independence, and the transfer to the Company of a right of ultimate control over those Courts, were not likely to increase their authority at least over Europeans.

Native agency in civil justice retained till 1772 under supervision.

But nevertheless, the administration for the most part of the revenues, and still more of civil justice, was conducted through native agency till the year 1772. The country in the neighbourhood of Calcutta, of Burdwan, Midnapore, and Chittagong was under the superintendence of the Company's European servants. But the remainder of the provinces, usually called the dewanny lands, were left under the immediate management of two native Dewans, one stationed at Moorshedabad, and the other at Patna. It was not thought prudent, either by the Local Government or by the Directors, to vest the immediate management of the revenue

* Mill's History of India, Vol. III., p. 363.

† *Ibid.*, p. 370.

LECTURE II.

or the administration of justice in the European servants. It is doubtful whether the Europeans at that time possessed sufficient knowledge of the civil institutions and the interior state of the country to qualify them for the trust.

The Company's supervision thereof.

A resident * at the Nabob's Court, who inspected the management of the Moorshedabad Dewan, and an officer of a similar position at Patna, who superintended the collections by a native of rank of the province of Behar, maintained an imperfect control over the civil administration of the Company's grants; while the zemindary lands of Calcutta and the twenty-four Pergunnahs, and the ceded districts of Burdwan, Midnapore, and Chittagong, which at an earlier period had been obtained by special grant from the Nabob of Bengal, were superintended by the covenanted servants of the Company.

Authority of native Dewans.

Mohamed Reza Khan was the Dewan at Moorshedabad, and Shitab Roy at Patna; and they had till 1769 almost exclusive direction of all details relative to the settlement and collections of the districts in Bengal and Behar, and therefore of the administration of civil justice; under the superintendence at their respective headquarters of a European resident.

Supervision gradually extended.

The work of supervision thus commenced was gradually extended until the Company was able to take into its own hands the work which it at first entrusted to the native authorities. In 1769 European local supervisors, in subordination to the two residents, were appointed; chiefly, no doubt, with a view to the revenue, but also in order to superintend the judicial administration. In the next† year, 1770, two revenue councils of control, with superior authority, were appointed, one at Moorshedabad, and the other at Patna.

* See 5th Report of Select Committee of House of Commons, dated 28th July, 1812, and 2 Harrington's Analysis, p. 2, *note*.

† 2 Harrington's Analysis, p. 6.

With regard to criminal justice, that also was left in the hands of native authorities, subject to the occasional control of the supervisors and councils just mentioned. Mahomedan criminal law was in force throughout the country, administered by Mahomedan Courts.

Native agency in criminal justice retained.

At first but little alteration was made in the existing system. The same law was continued in force, and the same tribunals were charged with its administration. In the presidency town* the judicial authorities were:—1. The Nabob himself in all capital cases. 2. His deputy in cases of quarrels, frays, and abusive names. 3. The Foujdar in all cases not capital, judgment and sentence being passed by the Nabob. 4. The Mohtesil in all cases of drunkenness, selling spirituous liquors, &c. 5. The Cotwal, a peace officer of the night, dependent on the Foujdaree. In the provinces the zemindars exercised civil and criminal jurisdiction over their several districts. In capital cases they reported to the Nazim; in others they were practically uncontrolled.

The utter inefficiency of this system to ensure protection to life and property soon became manifest. It was probably impossible for the English at once to assume the duty of administering criminal justice themselves, and the native Courts were without any authority, except such as they exercised by the sufferance of the dominant party. Those who had the power were obliged eventually to assume responsibility, and the first steps towards that end were gradually to undertake the work of supervision. A severe famine which raged in Bengal in 1770 led indirectly to a change of policy and to the scheme which was announced in the following year of a more direct and active exercise of authority.

Change of policy.

In 1771 the Directors declared their† resolution "to stand

* Beaufort's Criminal Digest, p. 4.

† Communicated in their letter to the President and Council at

LECTURE II.

forth as Dewan and by the agency of the Company's servants to take upon themselves the entire care and management of the revenues." This involved the entire remodelling of rights of property in the soil and the assumption of the administration of justice. It expressed the policy which had already been determined upon, *viz.*, to abandon the government though the Nabob's hierarchy of officials subject to English supervision, and to transfer to the Company's servants the direct discharge of the duties of administration.

The Company undertake the administration of civil justice.

The next event was that Warren Hastings was transferred from Madras to the Governorship of Bengal, where he landed early in 1772. The office of Naib Dewan was abolished, and the efficient administration of the internal government was at last undertaken by British agency;* though many years were yet to elapse before native agency could be dispensed with. Immediate measures were taken for the regular distribution of justice. A committee of circuit was appointed, consisting of the Governor and four members of Council, the report of which was drawn up by Warren Hastings. It drew attention to the inefficiency of the Mahomedan law Courts then existing, and proposed a plan which was immediately adopted by the Government, under which Mofussil Dewanny Adawluts, or Provincial Courts of Civil Justice, superintended by Collectors of the Revenue, were established in each district. These Courts took cognizance of all disputes, real or personal, all causes of inheritance, marriage, and caste, and all claims of debt, disputed accounts, contracts and demands of rent. Questions of succession to the zemindary and talookdaree property were not submitted to these Mofussil or Collectors' Courts, but were reserved for the decision of the Governor in Council.

Fort William, dated 28th August, 1771; see 1 Harrington's Analysis, p. 8, *note*.

* 1 Harrington's Analysis, p. 8.

Also of criminal justice.

With reference to criminal jurisdiction, the Mahomedan law and Mahomedan officers of justice were continued, but the whole plan was changed. A Court of Criminal Judicature was established in each district, called a Foujdaree Adawlut. In it a Kazee and a Mooftee, with the assistance of two Moulvies, appointed to expound the law, sat to hold trials for all criminal offences.* The English Collectors of Revenue were, however, directed to superintend the proceedings of those Courts, to see that the necessary witnesses were summoned and examined; that due weight was allowed to their testimony; and that the decisions passed were fair and impartial.

Chief Criminal Court.

These Foujdaree Adawluts were placed under the control of a Sudder Nizamut Adawlut established at Moorshedabad. It was presided over by a Darogah or chief officer, appointed by the Nizam. A chief Kazee, a chief Mooftee, and three Moulvies sat to assist him. The duty of the Court was † "to revise all the proceedings of the Foujdaree Adawluts; and in capital cases, by signifying their approbation and disapprobation thereof, with their reasons at large, to prepare the sentence for the warrant of the Nazim." An English committee of revenue was at first placed at Moorshedabad to control the proceedings of the Court, in order to prevent the perversion of the course of justice. The Court, however, was shortly after its establishment on its new basis removed to Calcutta, to be more immediately under the superintendence of the President and Council; and the committee, apparently, was then abolished. In 1775 the Court was removed back again to Moorshedabad, where it remained for fifteen years, the Nazim having the entire control over the department of criminal justice.

Chief Civil Court.

Besides the Criminal Court of Appeal, a Sudder Dewanny

* See preamble to Regulation IX. of 1793.

† Beaufort's Criminal Digest, p. 5.

Lecture II.

Adawlut was also established, and, like the Criminal Court, presided over by the President and Members of Council, assisted by native officers. It exercised appellate civil jurisdiction over the Mofussil Courts in all cases where the disputed amount exceeded Rs. 500.

Character of Warren Hastings' plan of 1772.

This was the general character of the scheme devised by the Government of Warren Hastings, and it has often been warmly approved. The adoption of the policy indicated by that scheme, and the assumption of the direct responsibility of government in lieu of a mere plan of partial supervision of the Nabob's officers, has sometimes been called a dissolution of the double government instituted by Lord Clive. That is one way of regarding it; but on the other hand, the administration of justice was carried on in the name of the Nabob and by his officers for the next eighteen years, during fifteen of which the Chief Court of Criminal Appeal was stationed at Moorshedabad under his immediate control. It seems to me that it was merely intended to be a considerable step towards a reorganization of the country, and that Warren Hastings had as little intention to dissolve, as Lord Clive to found, a double government. Both of those statesmen recognized that all real authority was vested in the Company. Both for political reasons determined that the name and shadow of authority should remain with the Mogul and his lieutenant. Mahomedan law, law officers, and revenue officials were retained, but were gradually replaced by the Company's regulations and servants. Seven years of supervision and inquiry, and greater knowledge of the country and its inhabitants, rendered it practicable to substitute the scheme of 1772 for the tax gathering and partial supervision of the preceding years. The decisive step of bringing Warren Hastings to Calcutta, and of standing forth as Dewan, both of which measures proceeded from the Directors, may have been stimulated by a knowledge of what was passing in the public mind at home, and of the probable measures which Parliament might think necessary to adopt in order to discharge the duties of government which had been assumed and neglected.

Interference of English Government and public opinion.

A variety of circumstances had tended to draw the attention of the English public to the state of Indian affairs. The general unpopularity of the returned servants of the Company, their wealth and ostentation, attracted attention, and induced the public mind to believe that the sudden creation of this wealthy class was due to great crimes and great oppression. The strong prejudices thus excited served to strengthen the hands of a few English statesmen, amongst them conspicuously Edmund Burke, who had been roused by the tales of cruelty and oppression which had reached the public ear, and who determined to bring the authority of Parliament into action to restrain the excesses of their countrymen abroad, and to secure some measure of protection and good government to the territories which they had acquired.

Policy of the Directors.

In 1769 the East India Company, disappointed with their expectations of profit, had resolved to send three supervisors to India to control, and, if necessary, to supersede the authority of the President in Council. But, notwithstanding every attempt to evade the rights of the Crown, public opinion was gradually acquiring strength, and a committee of secrecy of the House of Commons was appointed in 1772 to carry out the general demand for investigation. As the result thereof, the Company was prevented from sending out the supervisors. Another apparent result was the rejection of a Bill brought into the House of Commons by Mr. Sullivan for the due administration of justice in Bengal. Mr. Sullivan was Deputy Chairman of the Company, and the celebrated rival and antagonist of Lord Clive on the Board of Directors. According to its provisions, a new Court was to have been

Lecture II.

established in Bengal, the Judges to be appointed by the Company, and all Christian persons were to have been subject to its jurisdiction, and to have been exempted from the Courts of the Nabob.* This project, which would have concentrated all judicial power in the hands of the Company, failed.

Policy of Parliament.

The English Government appear by this time to have determined to interfere directly with the authority of the Company, and to assume the exercise of the sovereign powers which had been conceded by the Mogul. With reference to the administration of justice, they were strengthened in their determination by the result of their enquiries.

For the committee† of secrecy previously alluded to, reported in 1773, with reference to the Courts of Justice which had been established by the Mahomedan Government in Bengal, that, "so far as they were able to judge from all the information laid before them, the subjects of the Mogul Empire in that province derived little protection or security from any of these Courts; and that in general, though forms of judicature were established and preserved, the despotic principles of the Government rendered them the instruments of power rather than of justice; not only unavailing to protect the people, but often the means of the most grievous oppressions under the cloak of the judicial character."

The Regulating Act.

Accordingly in the same year an important Act of Parliament was passed "for establishing certain regulations for the better management of the affairs of the East India Company, as well in India as in Europe," which has been commonly called the Regulating Act.‡ It recited the Charter which established the Mayors' Courts, "which said Charter does not sufficiently provide for the administration of justice in such

* See Governor Johnstone's Speech, 30th March, 1772, referred to in Sir Charles Grey's Minute.

† Harrington's Analysis, Vol. I., p. 27.

‡ 13 Geo. III., c. 63.

manner as the state and condition of the Company's Presidency of Fort William in Bengal do and must require."

Provisions for Executive Government.

One subject with which the statute dealt was the constitution of the Governor-General's Council. It provided that the Government of Bengal should consist of a Governor-General and four Councillors, a majority to decide; and that the Presidents and Councils of Madras and Bombay should be Subordinate to the Governor-General and Council of Bengal, who were thereby constituted the Supreme Government in India, subject, however, to the Court of Directors in England.

For legislation.

By the 36th Section that Supreme Government was empowered "from time to time to make and issue such rules, ordinances, and regulations for the good order and civil Government of the United Company's settlement at Fort William, and other factories and places subordinate thereto, as shall be deemed just and reasonable (such rules, ordinances, and regulations not being repugnant to the laws of the nation), and to impose reasonable fines and forfeiture for the breach and non-observance thereof."

Such regulations, however, were not to be valid or of any force until they were duly registered in the Supreme Court, with the consent and approbation of the Court. An appeal from a regulation so registered and approved lay to the King in Council, but the pendency of such appeal was not allowed to hinder the immediate execution of the law. The Government were bound to forward all such rules and regulations to England, power being reserved to the King to disapprove them at any time within two years.

For establishment of Supreme Court.

The same Act also established the Supreme Court, leaving out the distinction of Christians, insisted upon by Mr. Sullivan, and placing in lieu thereof as the only criterion of personal liability to the jurisdiction that of subjection to the British Crown. By Section 14, all who are "His Majesty's

LECTURE II.

subjects" were made liable. The Judges were appointed by the Crown, and it was made a King's Court, and not a Company's Court.

The establishment of the Supreme Court was, in fact, the triumph of the party in England which desired greater intervention by the English Government and Parliament in Indian affairs and greater control over the Company's proceedings. The Company desired the establishment of a system of Courts which, from the highest to the lowest, should be under their own control. The intention of the dominant party apparently was to separate the judicial entirely from the executive branch of administration, and to reserve the former entirely to the Crown. They commenced with the establishment of a Supreme Court in Bengal, which apparently, it was hoped, would, with aid from England, in time draw into its own hands the whole supervision of inferior Courts, and the whole administration of justice.

The provisions of the Act which relate to the constitution of the Supreme Court are as follows:—The 13th Section empowered the King in Council by his Charter to establish the Court in Bengal, to consist of a Chief Justice and three Judges (*subsequently reduced to a Chief Justice and two Judges) who were to be appointed by the Crown and to be barristers of England or Ireland of not less than five years' standing. By the same Section it was declared that the Court should have power to exercise all civil, criminal, admiralty, and ecclesiastical jurisdiction, and to establish rules of practice and process, and to do all things necessary for the administration of justice. It was also declared that it should be a Court of Record, and a Court of Oyer and Terminer and Gaol Delivery for the town of Calcutta and factory of Fort William, and the factories subordinate thereto.

* See 37 Geo. III., Chap. 142, Sec. 1.

In pursuance of this Act, a Royal Charter, dated March 26, 1774, was granted, under which the Supreme Court of Calcutta was established, and continued to administer justice for the period of eighty-eight years. The extent of the jurisdiction of that Court was defined by the 13th Clause of the Charter, which authorized it to try all actions and suits concerning trespasses or injuries, or debts, or concerning any houses, lands, or other real or personal property in Bengal, Behar, or Orissa brought against the East India Company, the Mayor, and Aldermen of Calcutta, and "against any other of our subjects who shall be resident within the said provinces, districts, or provinces called Bengal, Behar, and Orissa, or who shall have resided there, or who shall have any debts, effects or estate, real or personal, within the same," and against persons employed directly or indirectly by the Company, the Mayor or Aldermen, or "any of our subjects." It could also try all actions or suits against every inhabitant of India residing in Bengal, Behar, and Orissa, upon any written contract with any of His Majesty's subjects where the cause of action exceeded Rs. 500, and when the contract provided that the Court should have jurisdiction. The Charter also provided the mode in which the Sheriff of Calcutta and his successors should be for the future appointed; and authorized them to execute all process of the Court, and to receive and detain in prison such persons as should be committed to him for that purpose by the Court.

The Charter.

Its jurisdiction as a Common Law Court.

The Supreme Court was also constituted a Court of Equity as the Court of Chancery in England. It was also constituted a Court of Oyer and Terminer and Gaol Delivery for Calcutta and Fort William and the factories subordinate thereto, with power to summon grand and petit juries, and to administer criminal justice as in the Courts of Oyer and Terminer in England with jurisdiction over all offences committed in Bengal, Behar, and Orissa, by any subject of His Majesty or

As an Equity Court.

As a Criminal Court.

Lecture II.

any person in the service of the United Company, or of any of the King's subjects.

As an Ecclesiastical Court.

The Court was also empowered to exercise ecclesiastical jurisdiction in Bengal, Behar, and Orissa towards and upon British subjects then residing in the same manner as it is exercised in the diocese of London, "so far as the circumstances and occasions of the said provinces or people shall admit or require;" and to grant probates and administrations to the estates of British subjects dying within the said provinces. The Court was also empowered to appoint guardians of infants and of insane persons and of their estates.

As an Admiralty Court.

It was also appointed to be a Court of Admiralty for the provinces of Bengal, Behar, and Orissa, "and all other territories and islands adjacent thereunto, and which are or ought to be dependent thereupon," with power to hear and determine all causes and matters, civil and maritime, and to have jurisdiction in crimes maritime, according to the course of the Admiralty in England.

Appeals from the Court to the Privy Council.

In civil cases an appeal lay to the Privy Council in such manner and form and under such rules as were observed in appeals from plantations or colonies, or from the Islands of Jersey, Guernsey, Sark, and Alderney. In criminal cases power of appeal was also given, but subject to considerable restrictions.

Both the Act of Parliament and the Charter which was granted in pursuance of it provided that the former Charter of the 26th of Geo. II. should become null and void, so far as the Mayor's Court in Fort William was concerned. Thus the Supreme Court was the only tribunal in the country, with the exception of the Court of Requests and a few inferior authorities, which owed its existence to the English Crown. The Adawluts established under the plan of Warren Hastings derived their authority from the Company, whether acting under the powers derived from the Mogul, or as the *de facto* masters of the country.

Indefinite terms of the Act and Charter.

Besides the inconveniences arising from political power being vested in a majority of council, instead of in a responsible governor, there were serious omissions, whether intentional or otherwise, in the provisions regarding the Supreme Court. Although the Act was intended to be the basis of a general settlement of Indian affairs, in a very few years its policy was entirely reversed, and its leading features swept away. The criticism of some later Judges of the Supreme Court upon it was "that * the Legislature had passed it without fully investigating what it was that they were legislating about; and that if the Act did not say more than was meant, it at least said more than was well understood."

For instance, subjection to the English Crown was made the ground of liability to the jurisdiction of the Court. But "there was not," as Sir Charles Grey points out,† "either in the Statute or in the Charter any declaration who are and who are not subjects, nor whether any of the territorial acquisitions amounted to an acquisition of the territory itself, or to anything more than powers to be exercised within territories of the Mogul, nor whether even Calcutta itself was so much within the allegiance that persons born there would be natural-born subjects of the British Crown." Those questions which were all of the greatest importance were left doubtful to be decided by the Court, whenever they might arise. Subject to such decision, the jurisdiction given to the Court was,‡ "first, over all persons whatsoever during their residence in any

* See 5th Appendix to 3rd Report of Select Committee of the House of Commons, 1831, p. 1234.

† *Ibid.*, p. 1143.

‡ *Ibid.*, p. 1234.

British territory, possession, or factory within Bengal, Behar, or Orissa; secondly, over all natural-born subjects or others having indefeasibly the character of subjects of the British Crown; and over persons in their service within Bengal, Behar, or Orissa, whether the place in which they might be were a British territory, possession, or factory, or a place belonging to some Indian prince, but under the protection of the Company. The intention was to have secured to the Crown a supremacy in the whole administration of justice, but the provisions made were inadequate to the attainment of the object, and have been defeated."

Relation of the Court to the Council.

Thus there were established in India two independent and rival powers, *viz.*, of the Supreme Council and of the Supreme Court; the boundaries between them being utterly undefined, one deriving its authority from the Crown, and the other from the Company. For seven years the conflict between them raged. The Court issued its writs extensively throughout the country, arrested and brought to Calcutta all persons against whom complaints were lodged, zemindars, farmers, and occupiers of land, whatever their rank or consequence in the country. Defaulters to the revenue were set at liberty on *habeas corpus;* the government of the Nabob, which still remained in the hands of the Company, the effectual instrument for the administration of Criminal Justice was declared by the Court to be "an empty name, without any legal right, or the exercise of any power whatsoever;" * and the production in Court of papers containing the most secret transactions of Government was insisted upon. The Court was charged with stopping the wheels of Government by the technicalities of English law, and of effecting a total dissolution of social order.

* Mill's History of India, Vol. IV., p. 223.

Powers of the Court, and conduct of the Judges.

Although it is impossible to defend the acts of the Judges, it must be remembered that their position was from the first antagonistic to the Council; and that they carried out in India a scheme which had been prepared in England without adequate information or competent skill for the purpose of checking the excesses of administration and of re-establishing order on principles totally strange to the inhabitants. The essential character and object of that scheme were to weaken the power of the Government by vesting it in the hands of a majority, and to plant in its neighbourhood a Court, framed after the fashion of the existing Courts in England, with jurisdiction over all its executive acts and a veto on all its legislation. This tribunal, vested with such extraordinary powers, and so ludicrously unsuited to the social and political condition of Bengal, was not merely to exercise a civil and criminal jurisdiction, wholly strange and repugnant to the Indian people; it might sit one day on its common law side and give judgment to a suitor, and on the next day might sit on its equity side, and restrain that suitor from proceeding to execution. It might on one side adjudge a man to be the absolute owner of property, and on the other side consign him to perpetual imprisonment if he did not, in his character of trustee, forthwith give it up to those beneficially entitled. In short, the whole system of English law and equity, with its rules and customs and process, handed down from feudal times, moulded during struggles between secular and ecclesiastical powers, between church and commonalty, between common law and civil jurisprudence; which time alone had rendered endurable to the people amongst whom it had grown up, a people widely different in habits, character, and form of civilization from any to be found in the East, was introduced into India, not intentionally as a burden, but for its benefit and salvation.

The result.

The result was that the Court exercised large powers

Lecture II.

independently of Government, often so as to obstruct it, and had a complete control over legislation. Political power was thus vested in Judges who had neither the responsibilities nor the machinery of government. Such a system could not endure under any circumstances. Although the Courts are independent of Government in England, both are absolutely subordinate to the Legislature, in which, however, the power of Government predominates. To make the Legislature subordinate to the Court, instead of the Court subordinate to the Legislature, and at the same time to direct it to enforce a system of law utterly inapplicable to India, independently of or in opposition to the Government, which was at the same time weakened by divisions purposely created, appears to be the most destructive and pernicious policy that wit could devise. Although the judicial service should be independent of the executive, yet it must be subordinate to the Legislature, and legislation must be, if power and responsibility are to go together, the unfettered expression of sovereign authority, wherever that authority may reside, or from whatever source it be derived, whether from an electoral body or an absolute prince.

Failure of the Court.

The plan of controlling the Company's government by the King's Court entirely failed. The tribunal came to be regarded by the Natives, for whose protection it was established, with the utmost abhorrence. The policy which shaped the Regulating Act was, no doubt, well-intentioned, but it was rashly and ignorantly executed. None of the Parliaments of George III. were remarkable for their wisdom; but it was reserved for the Parliament which sat in 1773 by its Colonial Customs Policy and its Regulating Act to throw the affairs of two hemispheres into confusion. It endeavoured to rule America on the principle of parliamentary taxation, and to control the government of India by the operation of English law Courts. The result was that British power in the West was subverted, and in the East was for a time seriously endangered. The anarchy which ensued continued till the policy of the Regulating Act was reversed, and Indian society assumed the form which it retained till the Company and the Mogul Empire vanished.

LECTURE III.

EARLY HISTORY: THE SETTLEMENT OF 1781.

Consequences of the Regulating Act—Political events immediately preceding it—The new Council—Its dissensions—First exercise of power by the Supreme Court—Character of its proceedings—Consequences thereof—Upon the Revenue and Civil Justice—Upon Criminal Justice—Proceedings of the Court against individuals—Proceedings of the Court against the authorities—Crisis of the disputes—Conduct of Parliament—Conduct of the Company—Conduct of the Judges—They did not exceed their jurisdiction—Act of 1781—Limits set to the jurisdiction of the Supreme Court—The Governor-General and Council excepted therefrom—English Law no longer applicable to Natives—Power to frame suitable process—Recognition of the Provincial Courts—Indemnity—The Settlement of 1781—Indefiniteness of the jurisdiction—Distinction between Presidency Towns and Mofussil perpetuated—Conclusion.

Consequences of Regulating Act.

THE Bengal Government and the English Parliament had thus in 1774, by their combined efforts, established a political and judicial system in the Lower Provinces. The events of the next seven years showed clearly that, whether from the antagonism of the local authorities, or from inherent faults, the provisions of the Regulating Act were unsuited to the wants of the country. Those events deserve some study and consideration, as they throw considerable light on the subsequent history and account for the crude and unsatisfactory condition in which the judicial, if not the legislative, institutions of the country were placed for very nearly a century.

Political events immedi-

Before the arrival of the Regulating Act, Mahomed Reza Khan and Shitab Roy, the two dewans of Moorshedabad and

Patna, had been removed by the Governor from their positions of authority and trust. Nuncoomar, the celebrated Brahmin of Bengal, had for some time been the implacable enemy of the former, but had lately transferred his animosity to Mr. Hastings. The subjugation of the Rohillas, both as to its policy and the manner in which that policy was executed, gave rise to serious questions as to the conduct of the Government.

ately preceding it.

The new Council.

Mr. Hastings was named in the Act Governor-General, with Mr. Barwell, an experienced Indian Administrator, as one of his Councillors; but three Englishmen, new to India and its politics, General Clavering, Mr. Monson, and Mr. Francis, were also appointed to outvote him in his own Council. Sir Elijah Impey, as Chief Justice of the Supreme Court, arrived with three Puisne Judges, to exercise an immense and undefined civil and criminal jurisdiction. The majority of the Council took the government into their own hands, condemned and reversed the previous policy of the Governor-General; interfered in the affairs of Madras and Bombay, and in the intestine disputes of the Mahratta Government. "At the same time * they fell on the internal administration of Bengal, and attacked the whole fiscal and judicial system, a system which was undoubtedly defective, but which it was very improbable that gentlemen, fresh from England, would be competent to amend. The effect of their reform was that all protection to life and property was withdrawn, and that gangs of robbers plundered and slaughtered with impunity in the very suburbs of Calcutta." †

Its dissensions.

One result of the confusion thus introduced was that Nuncoomar, seeing that the power of the Governor-General was at an end, stood forth to accuse him of having been bribed to dismiss Mahomed Reza Khan and other offenders

* See Macaulay's Essays, Vol. III., p. 365.

† See further, Lectures VII. and VIII.

Lecture III.

with impunity, and of having sold several public offices. The notorious Francis, one of the most malignant and impracticable men that ever meddled with public affairs in England or in India, read the paper of accusation at the Council Board in presence of the Governor-General, and also a communication from Nuncoomar requesting to be heard in support of his accusation. The Governor-General refused to be confronted with an accuser at his own Council Board, and also to allow his Councillors to sit in judgment upon him. He accordingly dissolved the meeting and departed. The majority voted Clavering into the chair, called in Nuncoomar, and decided to go on with the charges. With dissensions of this grave character in the Executive Council, all government was practically at an end, and public affairs were at a dead lock. It is impossible to believe that in any country but Bengal, cowed by disaster and decimated by famine, the footing of conquerors who governed in this spirit could have been maintained.

First exercise of power by the Supreme Court.

With the counsels of the Executive thus divided and distracted, the Supreme Court first put forward its new authority; and to the astonishment of the Natives, an executive government, armed with despotic power, was baffled and vanquished by a Court of Justice, which sat in the neighbourhood, and to which no executive or administrative functions had been assigned. In the history of Bengal, Courts had always been subject to the Government, and were the instruments of its will and pleasure, alike in collecting revenue, inflicting punishment, and deciding disputes. Nuncoomar was supported by the whole force of the Executive, and doubtless fancied himself secure. But he was suddenly arrested, and committed to the common gaol, on a charge of having six years previously forged a bond. The Council protested and remonstrated, but a jury of the Supreme Court convicted, and Nuncoomar was sentenced to be hanged, and was accordingly executed. He deserved his fate; but in the machinations and intrigues which terminated so fatally for him, his miscalculations were due entirely to an utter incapacity to understand the nature of the new power which had been established in his country. His death showed to his countrymen that thereafter the possession of political power, and the support of the Executive, were no protection against this new and powerful tribunal.

Although the trial of Nuncoomar was regarded with very different feelings by the two factions in the Council, yet in the long contest which subsequently ensued between the Council on the one side, and the Court on the other, it is remarkable that both factions were unanimous in every step that was taken. It was the one subject upon which Hastings and Francis were in accord. In no country were two powers ever placed side by side so utterly irreconcilable.

Character of its proceedings.

The Court issued its writs against the zemindars of the country at the suit of private persons; zemindars were ordered to Calcutta; and if they neglected the writ, they were seized upon their estates, and forcibly brought up to the Presidency. They were there compelled to give bail, or else were consigned to the goal, which seems to have been a place unfit for the habitation of human beings, and were detained during the progress of the suit. Arrest to an Indian of rank is the deepest degradation, but the Supreme Court, as an English tribunal administering English law, did not take into consideration either the circumstances of the country or the feelings of the Natives to such a degree as to abolish any rule of procedure and of law which it was established in order to administer. "And," says Mr. Mill,* speaking of the law and procedure as they existed at the time the Supreme Court was founded, "the language of that law, its studied intricacies and obscurities which render it unintelligible to all English-

* Mill's History of India, Vol. IV., p. 220.

LECTURE III.

men who have not devoted a great part of their lives to the study of it, rendered it to the eye of the affrighted Indian a black and portentious cloud, from which every terrific and destructive form might at each moment be expected to descend upon him. Whoever is qualified to estimate the facility and violence with which alarms are excited among a simple and ignorant people, and the utter confusion with which life to them appears to be overspread, when the series of customs and rules by which it was governed is threatened with subversion may form an estimate of the terrors which agitated the Natives of India when the process of the Supreme Court began to operate extensively among them."

Consequences thereof.

The absence of so many zemindars (an affidavit of any Native being sufficient to procure a writ) struck a serious blow at the collection of revenue. Moreover, the Dewanny Adawluts were in the habit of enforcing claims for rent and revenue by a summary process. But the Supreme Court began to interfere with their coercive process; and their writs of *Habeas Corpus* were an additional source of embarrassment to the members of Government. Their interference destroyed the authority of the Provincial Courts, and rendered the collection of revenue a thing almost impossible.

Upon the revenue and civil justice.

Again, the whole administration of criminal justice was in the hands of the government of the Nabob, and carried out by its agency and authority. The Supreme Court declared that they would not recognize that government, and that their jurisdiction extended over all the dominions of the Nabob.

Upon criminal justice.

A summary is thus given of some of the proceedings of the Court*:—

Proceedings of the Court against individuals.

"Persons confined by the Courts of Dewanny Adawlut are collusively arrested by process from Calcutta, or removed by *Habeas Corpus* where the language is as unknown as the

* Mill's History of India, Vol. IV., p. 237.

power of the Court. The process is abused to terrify the people; frequent arrests made for the same cause; and there is an instance of the purchaser of a zemindary near Dacca who was ruined by suits commenced by paupers, suits derived from claims prior to his purchase, and who was at last condemned in considerable damages for an ordinary act of authority in his station. Hence the Natives of all ranks become fearful to act in the collection of revenues. The renters and even hereditary zemindars are driven away, or arrested at the time of the collections, and the crops embezzled. If a farm is sold on default of payment, the new farmer is sued, ruined, and disgraced. Ejectments are brought for land decreed in the Dewanny Adawlut. A talookdar is ruined by the expense of pleading to the jurisdiction, though he prevails. And in an action where Rs. 400 were recovered, the cost exceeded 1,600 rupees. When to these abuses incident to the institution of the Court itself, and derived from distance and the invincible ignorance of the Natives respecting the laws and practice of the Court, we add the disgrace brought on the higher orders, it will not perhaps be rash to affirm that confusion in the provinces and a prodigious loss of revenue must be the inevitable consequence of upholding this jurisdiction. One zemindar upon pretence that he had been arrested, and afterwards rescued, has his house broken open, and even the apartments of his women rudely violated. Another zemindar surrenders himself to prison to avoid the like disgrace to his family."

Proceedings of the Court against the authorities.

Prosecutions were carried on by the Supreme Court against the Judges of the Revenue and Civil Courts for acts done in the regular performance of their business, and by these means the course of justice was entirely suspended. "Who are the Provincial Chief and Council of Dacca?" asked the Supreme Court in reference to the governing body of a great province. "They are no *corporation* in the eye of

LECTURE III.

the law. The Chief and Provincial Council of Dacca is an ideal body. A man might as well say he was commanded by the King of the Fairies as by the Provincial Council of Dacca, because the law knows no such body." They held also that Native Magistrates, who were appointed by the Provincial Councils to investigate cases, were liable in damages at the suit of every person affected by their proceedings.

In 1777, the Supreme Court entertained an action for trespass and false imprisonment against the dewan or principal officer of the Criminal Court at Dacca. The action was brought by a peon who had been convicted in that Court and imprisoned. The Supreme Court ordered the defendant to be arrested, that last disgrace to a Mahomedan of rank. The bailiff entered the house of the Judge, and attempted to seize the dewan. He was prevented, and thereupon attended by a crowd, he broke open the gate of the house, and in the affray the Judge was dangerously wounded. It ended by the Provincial Council giving bail for the dewan. "All criminal justice," said the Governor-General in Council, "is at a stand and seems not likely to be resumed. How can a Judge perform any function of his office? How presume to execute a criminal convicted and sentenced to death by the established laws of the Government and his religion if he is liable himself to stand to actions of damages, or to answer to a criminal accusation according to the laws of England for any punishment he may inflict?"

The action of the Court was thus directed to render the management of the territorial revenue and the administration of civil and criminal justice subject to the jurisdiction of the King's Court. The Governor-General and Council declared that, by the acts and declarations of the Judges, the Company's office of dewan was annihilated; the country government subverted; and they and their officers, acting under their authority, were threatened with the pains and penalties of high treason. The Judges asserted that their power derived directly from the Crown was greater than that of the Council which was derived from the Company, and that their duty was by the inherent force and vigour of English law to restrain the Executive, and to protect the Natives. LECTURE III.

So general was the sense of oppression and insecurity that, in the Province of Behar, the farmers and land-owners petitioned the Governor in Council, praying for protection against the process of the Supreme Court, or if that could not be granted, for leave to relinquish their farms that they might retire into another country.

Crisis of the disputes.

The case in which the disputes reached a crisis was this. In 1779 the Rajah of Cossijurah absconded to avoid the execution of a writ of the Supreme Court. Another writ was issued to sequester his land and effects. Sixty men, headed by a serjeant of the Court, were sent to execute it. The Rajah complained that they entered his house, beat and wounded his servants, broke open and forcibly entered his zenana, stripped his place of religious worship of its ornaments, and prohibited his farmers from paying their rents. The Governor-General and Council instructed the Rajah not to obey the process of the Court, and ordered the troops to intercept the party of the Sheriff, and to detain them in custody till further orders. The Government also issued a notification to all zemindars and others in the three provinces that, except in the two cases of their being British servants, or bound by their own agreement, they were not to obey the process of the Court. The Supreme Court took proceedings against the Company's attorney and the officers who seized the Sheriff's party. The attorney was thrown into prison, and finally the Governor-General and Council were at last individually served with a summons at the suit of the decree-holder, whose process of execution they had disturbed. They

LECTURE III.

declined to appear, and a petition, signed by the principal British inhabitants in Bengal, went home to Parliament against the exercise which the Supreme Court was making of its power.

The rule of the Supreme Court is described by * Lord Macaulay as a reign of terror; "of terror heightened by mystery; for even that which was endured was less horrible than that which was anticipated. No man knew what was next to be anticipated from this strange tribunal; it came from beyond the black water, as the people of India with mysterious horror called the sea; it consisted of Judges not one of whom was familiar with the usages of the millions over whom they claimed boundless authority. Its records were kept in unknown characters; its sentences were pronounced in unknown sounds. * * * No Mahratta invasion had ever spread through the province such dismay as this inroad of English lawyers; all the injustice of former oppressors, Asiatic and Europeans, appeared as a blessing compared with the justice of the Supreme Court."

Conduct of Parliament.

This unexampled scene was the direct and inevitable result of the legislation which sought by introducing an offshoot from Westminster Hall in an unknown country, whose form of civilization, religion, and habits were inflexible from their age, and utterly strange to the English Parliament, to re-establish society with the aid of a foreign and totally inapplicable class of laws. The statesmen who adopted this policy, and framed the Regulating Act, were chiefly responsible for the consequences. The accusations which, in the bitterness of those times, were levelled against the Judges seem to have been disproved. They were the ministers of a system, carrying out the objects and purposes of their judicial existence.

No doubt the Court was directed by its charter to accommodate its process to the circumstances of the people and the

* Macaulay's Essays, Vol. III., p. 388.

country. This was done to some extent, but it must be remembered that to do so successfully required more co-operation and support from the Executive than the Court was likely to obtain or did in fact meet with. It excited and undoubtedly experienced great opposition from the servants of the Company.* The first obstacle which it encountered was the upholding of the Nizamut under the Nabob and his Native officers in a state of complete independence of it. The Chief Court of the Nizamut was transferred from Calcutta to Moorshedabad immediately after the Court began to exercise its powers. Probably, if Mr. Sullivan's Bill (see *ante*, p. 31) had passed, the Company would have brought the whole of the Native Courts into subordination to the Court established by it. And when the Supreme Court was substituted, the jurisdiction, similar to that of the King's Bench which was given to it, indeed its very title and the objects of the whole Charter, showed that it was supposed that there would have been inferior Courts subjected to its superintendence. A system corresponding to such intentions could not have been established without the cordial co-operation of the Governor-General and Council of the time, and probably it ought not to have been attempted but by very slow and cautious steps, and supplementary enactments must have been made for securing the Hindus and Mahomedans against an abrupt demolition of their customs and usages. But instead of any preparations of such a tendency, all things were maintained in a posture rather of opposition than merely of separation. It may be said, therefore, in justification of the Judges, that there was not that co-operation which they had expected from the Government; that the re-establishment in 1775 of the Nizamut at Moorshedabad in its old form was not a symptom of any inclination to promote that

Conduct of the Company.

* Sir C. Grey's Minute, see 5th Appendix to the Third Report of the Select Committee of the House of Commons (1831), p. 1145.

LECTURE III.

subordination of the Provincial Courts which was looked for, and which would have been gradually accomplished if the Supreme Court had been a Court of the Company.

Conduct of the judges.

And further, in criticizing the conduct of the Judges, some allowance must be made for the novelty of their position and their consequent ignorance of their relative and absolute duties. They were English lawyers sent out expressly to administer English law; they had been educated in a belief of its comprehensiveness and perfection.* "They knew nothing of India, had never heard of Hindu or Mahomedan law, and would have despised it if they had: they had been accustomed to know that gross abuses of law and justice prevailed in India, and they imagined it to be their first of duties to show that they would resolutely exert the powers which they thought that they possessed, for the extension of the principles of the only law which they conceived to be capable of protecting the interests of society. That they entertained a mistaken opinion of their own dignity and an equally unfounded contempt for the Company's functionaries originated in the same cause, and to ignorance may be referred the origin of their indiscretion and intemperance."

No doubt at the time great passions and animosity were excited, and charges were made against the Judges of exceeding their jurisdiction, and against Sir Elijah Impey in particular of gross dereliction of duty. But these charges will not bear examination; and the personal question in these days readily yields to the interest of the political situation.

They did not exceed their jurisdiction.

And with regard to exceeding their jurisdiction, that charge also in general cannot be sustained. The Act of 1781 was passed, not because the jurisdiction had been exceeded, but because it had been found difficult to exercise it without conflict with the Provincial Courts and the Government; in short, because the Act of 1773 had proved to be a ruinous

* Mill's History of India, Vol. IV., p. 242.

mistake. The 28th Section provides indeed an indemnity for the Governor-General in Council and the Advocate-General for their transgressions of the law in opposition to the Judges, but no such indemnity will be found to have been granted or required for the Judges themselves. Parliament, no doubt, felt that the Act had been a failure, not because it had been misapplied, but because it was wholly inapplicable and unsuited to the wants of the country.

Act of 1781.

The Act of 1781 (21 Geo. III. c. 70) was passed to explain and amend the Act of 1773, "and for the relief of certain persons imprisoned at Calcutta under a judgment of the Supreme Court, and also for indemnifying the Governor-General and Council and all officers who have acted under their orders of authority in the undue resistance made to the process of the Supreme Court." It recited that doubts and difficulties had arisen with regard to the provisions of the Act of 1773, and the Charter which had been issued under it, and that "by reason thereof dissension hath arisen between the Judges and the Governor-General and Council and the minds of many inhabitants subject to the Government have been disquieted with fears and apprehensions, and further mischief may possibly ensue from the said misunderstandings and discontents if a seasonable and suitable remedy be not provided." And then the preamble proceeded, "whereas it is expedient that the lawful Government of the provinces of Bengal, Behar, and Orissa should be supported, that the revenues thereof should be collected with certainty, and that the inhabitants should be maintained and protected in the enjoyment of all their ancient laws, usages, rights, and privileges."

Limits set to the jurisdiction of the Supreme Court.

It was expressly declared by that Act that the Supreme Court should not have any jurisdiction in any matter concerning the revenue or concerning any acts ordered or done in the collection thereof according to the practice of the country, or the regulations of the Governor-General and Council. Further,

LECTURE III.

it was declared that no person should be subject to its jurisdiction by virtue of possessing any interest in, or authority over, lands or rents within Bengal, Behar, or Orissa, or by reason of his becoming security for the payment of such rents. Employment of a person, directly or indirectly, by the Company, or the Governor-General and Council, or by a native of Great Britain, was declared not to subject such person to the jurisdiction of the Court in any matter of inheritance or succession to lands or goods, or in any matter of dealing or contract between party or parties, except in actions for wrongs or trespasses, and also except in any Civil suit by agreement of parties in writing to submit the same to the decision of the said Court. Further no action for wrong or injury should lie in the Supreme Court against any person whatsoever exercising a judicial office in the country Courts for any of his judicial decisions, nor against any person acting thereunder.

The Governor-General and Council excepted therefrom.

The former Act had declared the Supreme Court incompetent to try any indictment against the Governor-General or any of the Council for the time being for any offence not being treason or felony which such Governor or any of his Council should be charged with having committed in Bengal, Behar, or Orissa. The Governor-General and Council and Chief Justice and Judges were declared not to be liable to arrest or imprisonment upon any action, suit, or proceeding in the Court. The later Act declared that the Governor-General and Council should not be subject jointly or severally to the jurisdiction of the Supreme Court "for or by reason of any act or order, or any other matter or thing whatsoever, counselled, ordered, or done by them in their public capacity only and acting as Governor-General and Council." It was also provided that the order of the Governor-General and Council in writing should amount to a sufficient justification of all acts done thereunder; except that where British subjects were concerned, the Court should retain its jurisdiction.

English law no longer applicable to Natives.

With reference to the inconveniences which had arisen from applying English law to the Natives, the Supreme Court was, by the 17th Section of the new Act, empowered to determine all actions and suits against the inhabitants of the city of Calcutta: provided that their succession and inheritance to lands, rents, and goods, and all matters of contract and dealing between party and party, should be determined in the case of Mahomedans by the laws and usages of Mahomedans, and in the case of Gentoos by the laws and usages of Gentoos; and where only one of the parties should be a Mahomedan or Gentoo by the laws and usages of the defendant. And in order that regard should be had to the civil and religious usages of the Natives, it was enacted that the rights and authorities of fathers and masters of families, according as the same might have been exercised by the Gentoo or Mahomedan law, should be preserved to them; "nor shall any acts done in consequence of the rule and law of caste respecting the members of the said families only be held and adjudged a crime, although the same may not be held justifiable by the laws of England."

Power to frame suitable process.

It was also provided that the Supreme Court might frame such process and make such rules and orders for the execution thereof in suits, civil or criminal, against the Natives of the presidency as might accommodate the same to the religion and manners of the Natives, so far as the same might consist with the due execution of the laws and attainment of justice. Such rules and orders were to be subject to the royal approbation, correction, or refusal.

Recognition of the Provincial Courts.

But perhaps the most important part of the Act, and the one which most completely reversed the policy of the Act of 1773, was the recognition by Parliament of the Civil and Criminal Provincial Courts, existing independently of the

Supreme Court; and of the Governor-General and Council or some committee thereof, as the Chief Appellate Court of the country, and the vesting the Council with the power to frame Regulations for those Provincial Courts independently of the Supreme Court. The Sections are as follows:—

Section 21.—And whereas the Governor-General and Council, or some committee thereof, or appointed thereby, do determine on appeals and references from the country or Provincial Courts in civil causes, be it further enacted that the said Court shall and lawfully may hold all such pleas and appeals in the manner and with such powers as it hitherto hath held the same, and shall be deemed in law a Court of Record; and the judgments therein given shall be final and conclusive; except upon appeal to His Majesty, in civil suits only, the value of which shall be £5000 and upwards.

Section 22 gave the Court power to determine on all offences, abuses, and extortions committed in the collection of revenue, or of severities used beyond what was customary or necessary to the case, and to punish the same, provided the punishment should not extend to death or maiming, or perpetual imprisonment.

Section 23.—And it is hereby enacted that the Governor-General and Council shall have power and authority from time to time to frame Regulations for the Provincial Courts and Councils. A proviso was added that His Majesty in Council might disallow or amend them within two years.

Indemnity.

The Act also declared that no action should lie in the Supreme Court against any judicial officer in the country Courts in respect of any judgment or order of his Court, nor against any person for any act done in pursuance of such order; it being considered "reasonable to render the Provincial Magistrates, as well Native as British subjects, more safe in the execution of their office."

And finally, with regard to the indemnity in respect of the

hostilities which had been carried on between the Court and the Council, wherein said the Act "many things have been done not justifiable by the strict rule of the law," it was enacted that the Governor-General and Council and Advocate-General and all persons acting under their orders, so far as the same related to the resistance to any process of the Supreme Court from January 1, 1779, to January 1, 1780, were thereby indemnified, discharged, and saved harmless from any action, suit, or prosecution whatsoever on account of the said disobedience and resistance to the execution of the orders of the Court.

The Settlement of 1781.

Thus within eight years the main provisions of the Regulation Act were swept away. The Supreme Court, however, continued to exist, and ultimately, with its diminished powers and pretensions, won its way to greater authority and respect, both from Europeans and Natives, than any other tribunal which has ever existed in India. Nothing, however, in its subsequent history serves to justify or excuse the policy of its founders. Their attempt to introduce an English superintendence of law and justice on the part of the Crown, and an administration of English rules of law and equity by an English Court, modelled according to English fashion, was made rashly and ignorantly, without any sufficient scheme or due preparation; without any measures being taken to ensure the co-operation of the local authorities, but on the contrary with every attempt to impose upon them a policy to which they were opposed, and which they were determined to subvert.

Indefiniteness of the jurisdiction.

But in the Act of 1781, as in that of 1773, there is no plain statement of the relation in which the Indian territories stood to the British Crown, nor whether any Indian natives were to be comprehended under the term "subjects," nor whether* the Provincial Courts were to have a concurrent

* Sir C. Grey's Minute.

LECTURE III.

jurisdiction with the Supreme Court, or an exclusive one; nor, if the latter, what were to be the limits of it. The phrase "British subjects" is used in both Acts in such a way as necessarily to exclude from its meaning the Hindu and Mahomedan inhabitants; but it is so used that, with respect at least to subjects not being natives of Great Britain or India, subsequent glosses made it almost impossible to affix any definite understanding to it.

Distinction between Presidency Towns and Mofussil perpetuated.

The result of the two Acts was that the distinction between Presidency Towns and Mofussil which originated in the distinction between the Company's factories and the Mogul territory was perpetuated. At the distance of nearly a century (1872), it still exists. The influence of the Presidency Town system was, since the Act of 1781, but thinly scattered over the Mofussil, and the disputes and inconveniences which arose were temporary and occasional. The subsequent pages will show the steady progress which has, since the abolition of the Supreme Court in 1861, been made towards obliterating this distinction and securing uniformity in the administration of justice.

The Act of 1781 at all events settled the difficulties which had arisen under the Regulating Act, and the settlement, crude and unsatisfactory as it was, was copied in the other Presidencies, and endured so long as the Company and the Mogul Empire existed.

Conclusion.

In Bengal a revised Code was issued in the same year as this important Act. Very little legislation had been effected under the Regulating Act; though, under the Act of 1781, a large body of Regulations continued to be passed for half a century. Thus the Act of Parliament, the Revised Code, the Parliamentary recognition of the Sudder and Provincial Courts, the grant of legislative authority apart from the veto of the Supreme Court, the restriction of the powers of that Court, and the declaration of the right of Hindus and

Mahomedans to their own laws and usages, were effected in 1781. A complete settlement was made sufficient to form the foundation of the Indian polity for three generations, and to mark the commencement of a new era in Indian History. Lecture III.

In that era the Supreme Court acquired authority and renown; and English lawyers in India have laid the foundation of a complete system of Anglo-Indian jurisprudence. They have carried out the ultimate end and object of the Regulating Act—an object which has redeemed the character of the Statute and of its immediate policy—*viz.* to teach both rulers and subjects in the East that respect for law which is the foundation of social order and the greatest gift which England has had it in its power to bestow on India. The angry opposition which has been at times excited has died away, and as India is now united under a monarchy which is itself limited by law, and is settling down, even in its farthest provinces, into a law-governed country, the wishes of the authors of the Regulating Acts which they so utterly failed to accomplish may be said to have been ultimately fulfilled.

I shall now trace separately the history of the legislative authorities which have from time to time existed throughout India, of the Supreme Courts, and other judicial authorities established in the Presidency Towns, and of the Civil and Criminal Courts of the country. In eighty years we shall arrive at a new epoch, the date from which nearly all existing legislative and judicial authority derives its origin.

LECTURE IV.

THE LEGISLATIVE COUNCILS.

Two-fold power of legislation given—Extent of the first power—Extent of the second—Excessive exercise of the powers—Parliamentary recognition thereof—Mode of exercising legislative power prescribed—Legislative power at Madras—At Bombay and Madras—Extent of the power—Extension of legislative authority in 1813—Power of taxation—Jurisdiction of the Legislature—Regulations to be laid before Parliament—Reservation of Sovereignty of the Crown—Power to make Articles of War—Customs—Power to alter the revenue and impose new taxes—Statute Law in 1834—Necessity for reform in the Legislature—The Act of William the Fourth—Provisions relative to legislation—Indian Law Commissioners—Local Legislatures superseded—Articles of War—Conclusion.

Two-fold power of legislation given.

I HAVE already described the extent of the legislative power granted by Parliament to the Company during the early period which preceded the passing of the Regulating Act. The most important exercise of that power, whether within or in excess of its terms it is unnecessary now to enquire, occurred in 1772. In that year the President * and Council of Bengal made and ordained certain general regulations for the administration of justice, by virtue of which certain Courts, both Civil and Criminal, such as have already been described, were established throughout the Lower Provinces of Bengal, with certain definite rules of procedure and law.

The Act of 1773 defined the extent of the legislative authority of the Governor-General and Council, and placed

* See Colebrooke's Supplement to the Digest of Regulations, Vol. III., p. 1.

it under the supervision and subject to the veto of the Supreme Court. No enactments of any importance were passed till 1780, when the Governor-General and Council, considering that important changes had taken place in the constitution and civil government of those provinces since 1772, passed certain regulations * for the more effectual and regular administration of justice in the provincial Civil Courts. Those Regulations were to be considered binding only till a new arrangement should be made by authority of Parliament.†

Later in the same year it confirmed and amended all existing regulations respecting the Sudder and Provincial Courts. And early in 1781 a revised Code was issued.

These must be taken to have been passed in pursuance of the legislative power granted by the Regulating Act. They are not expressed to be registered in the Supreme Court, and probably were not so registered.

But in 1781 the new Act of Parliament (21 Geo. III. c. 70) empowered the Governor-General and Council to frame Regulations for the Provincial Courts, without reference to the Supreme Court. It was under that authority that the Government preferred to act. But they were unable to pass any Regulation which the Supreme Court was in any way bound to recognize, unless it was previously registered as directed by the Act of 1773.

Extent of the first power.

The Supreme Council, therefore, had from the first a two-fold power of legislation conferred by two separate Acts of Parliament. The one enabled them to make laws for the good order and civil government of the settlement at Fort William and all factories and places subordinate thereto, and to make any Regulations not repugnant to the laws of the

* See Colebrooke's Supplement to the Digest of Regulations, Vol. III., p. 14.

† *Ibid.*, p. 22.

LECTURE IV.

realm, and to enforce them by reasonable sanctions; but the exercise of the power was subject to the supervision of the Court. It has been said that the power so conferred was intended to apply only to Calcutta and its dependent factories, into which English law had already been introduced, and not to what are in that Act described as the territorial acquisitions of Bengal, Behar, and Orissa. But the Act does not appear to have been so understood; and the large body of regulation law mentioned above was framed in pursuance of its powers for the benefit of the provinces.

Extent of the second.

The second power of legislation was derived from the Act of 1781, by which the Governor-General and Council or some committee thereof or appointed thereby was empowered as a Court of Record to determine on appeals or references from the country or Provincial Courts in civil causes; and from time to time to frame Regulations for the Provincial Courts and Councils. Copies of such Regulations were to be transmitted within six months to the Court of Directors and to the Secretary of State, and if not disallowed within two years, they were to be of force and authority to direct the Provincial Courts. Power to disallow or amend such Regulations was reserved to the Sovereign in Council. It was under this Act that, notwithstanding the limited purpose it professed to have in view, most of the Regulation law was passed. The Supreme Court had no power of supervision or of veto in reference to any enactments passed in pursuance of this statute, and in consequence the Council preferred to legislate under its provisions in preference to those of the earlier Act. But the Court, on the other hand, was not in terms nor in effect bound by any Regulations which were not duly registered by it.

Registration of laws in the Supreme Court or in any Court of Justice was rendered unnecessary by the Act * of William IV. passed in 1833.

* 3 & 4 Wm. IV., c. 85, s. 45.

The Regulations passed in pursuance of the authority granted in 1781 were doubtless far in excess of the legislative power, having regard to the precise terms in which it was granted. But after several years of its exercise, Parliament itself * referred to that power as if it were one of making a regular Code affecting the rights, persons, and property of the Natives and others amenable to the Provincial Courts. That was a Parliamentary recognition of the power which the Indian Council had assumed to exercise. The Council, regardless of the limited extent of its legislative authority, had passed numerous Regulations; and in 1793 collected and passed them in the shape of a Revised Code.

Excessive exercise of the powers.

The Act of Parliament to which I have just alluded was passed in 1797. It recited that various Regulations for the better administration of justice among native inhabitants and others within the Provinces of Bengal, Behar, and Orissa were from time to time framed by the Governor-General in Council in Bengal. It recited, also, that it had been established as essential to the future prosperity of the British territories in Bengal that all Regulations passed by Government affecting the rights, properties, or persons of the subjects should be formed into a regular Code, and printed with translations in the country languages; that the ground of every Regulation should be prefixed to it; and that the Courts of Justice within the Provinces should be bound to regulate their decisions by the rules and ordinances which such Regulations might contain. Parliament referring to these proceedings considered that it was essential that so wise and salutary a provision should be strictly observed, and that it should not be in the power of any Governor-General in Council to neglect or dispense with it for the future.

Parliamentary recognition thereof

Accordingly† it was enacted that all the Regulations of that

Mode of exercising

* See 37 Geo. III., c. 142, s. 8.

† *Ibid.*

Lecture IV.

legislative power prescribed.

Council affecting the rights, property, or persons of the Natives, or of any other individuals who might be amenable to the Provincial Courts of Justice (thereby recognizing the full extent of the legislative authority which had been assumed and exercised), should be registered in the Judicial Department, and formed into a regular Code, and printed with translations in the country languages, and that the grounds of each Regulation should be prefixed to it. And all the Provincial Courts of Judicature were directed to be bound thereby, and to regulate their decisions accordingly. Copies of the Regulations were directed to be annually transmitted to the Court of Directors and to the Board of Commissioners. By this Act, therefore, the legislative power of the Governor-General, independently of the Supreme Court, was recognized and confirmed, and endeavours were made to place it under control. It was not, however, the first endeavour to place the legislative power in India under some restrictions; for George the First's Charter had reserved to the home authorities a power of supervision. But at this time a formal publication, a written record of reasons for resorting to particular enactments, and official communication of their contents to the authorities in England, were deemed to be necessary expedients for placing a check on any hasty exercise of power.

Legislative power at Madras.

The legislative power being thus firmly planted in Bengal, it next became necessary to establish a similar authority in the other Presidencies. Accordingly, in the year 1800 the Governor* and Council of Fort St. George at Madras were invested within the territories subject to their government with the same legislative power as had previously by any Act been given to the Governor-General and Council of Fort William, that is, they were empowered to frame Regulations for the Provincial Courts and Councils annexed to that Presidency.

* See 39 & 40 Geo. III., 79, s. 11.

Lecture IV.

At Bombay and Madras.

Again in 1807 an Act * was passed amongst other things "for the better government of the settlements of Fort St. George and Bombay." It recited the expediency of granting to the two local Governors in Council the same powers of government within their respective territories as were vested in the Governor-General and Council for the government of Fort William. It accordingly empowered them respectively from time to time to make and issue such rules and regulations for the good order and civil government of the towns of Madras and Bombay, and of the Company's settlements at Fort St. George and Bombay, and other factories subordinate thereto, and to add the necessary sanctions, as the Governor-General in Council might make for the good order and civil government of Fort William. But it provided that registration thereof in the Supreme Courts of Fort St. George and Bombay respectively should be necessary to their validity. Such regulations were to be subject to appeal as provided by existing Acts of Parliament.†

Extent of the power.

As these Acts of 1800 and 1807 were later than the Act of 1797, it might reasonably be considered that the local Governors and Councils had legislative powers conferred on them, not as defined by the Acts of 1773 and 1781, but as recognized and confirmed by the Act of 1797.

It does not appear that the Governor-General exercised any direct authority over the Governors in Council at Madras or Bombay in the matter of making laws. He had control over them in political matters under the Act of 1773, and in revenue matters and all cases whatever under the Act of 1797. A copy of every regulation passed at Madras and Bombay was sent to the Governor-General in Council; but it does not appear that it was submitted for approval before being passed. The legislative powers of the Governor-

* 47 Geo. III., sess. 2, c. 68.

† *Vide* 13 Geo. III., c. 63; and 39 & 40 Geo. III., c. 79.

LECTURE IV.

General's Council were confined by the terms of its constitution and in practice to the Presidency of Bengal.

Extension of legislative authority in 1813.

In 1813 the legislative power so conferred on all three Councils was extended, and at the same time placed under still greater control. The Governor-General and the Governors in Council in their respective Presidencies, with the sanction of the Court of Directors and the Board of Commissioners, were empowered by an Act * passed in that year to impose duties and taxes within the towns of Calcutta, Madras, and Bombay; for the enforcing of which taxes, regulations were directed to be made by the Governor-General and Governors in Council in the same manner as other regulations were made.

Power of taxation.

Jurisdiction of the Legislature.

It was also provided in the same Act † that the regulations should apply to all persons who should proceed to the East Indies within the limits of the Company's government.

Regulations to be laid before Parliament.

And in addition to the rule which had compelled the Indian Government to forward to the authorities in England copies of all regulations passed, it was then enacted ‡ that copies of legislative regulations, made by the several Governments of India, and required by various Acts of Parliament to be sent home, should be annually laid before Parliament.

Reservation of Sovereignty of the Crown.

Section 95 of the same Act enacted "that nothing in this Act contained shall extend or be construed to extend to prejudice or affect the undoubted sovereignty of the Crown of the United Kingdom of Great Britain and Ireland in and over the said territorial acquisitions."

Power to make Articles of War.

Then followed two Sections, one of which (Sec. 96) enabled all three Governments to make Articles of War for the order and discipline of the native officers and soldiers in their

* 53 Geo. III., c. 155, ss. 98, 99, and 100.

† Section 35.

‡ *Vide* Section 66.

respective service; and for the administration of justice by Courts Martial to be holden on such officers and soldiers; and for the constitution and manner of proceeding of such Courts Martial. LECTURE IV.

Customs.

Another Section (98) authorized them, with the sanction of the Home authorities, to impose, within the limits of their respective Presidencies, duties of customs and other taxes in respect of all goods and property and on all persons, British-born or foreigners, being therein.

Power to alter the revenue and impose new taxes.

In addition to those three powers of legislation conferred under the Acts of 1773, 1781, and 1813, a general power of altering the revenue, and of imposing new taxes, had been exercised within the provinces, and is alluded to more than once in Acts of Parliament. But as there is no Act which expressly conferred it, such power has generally been considered to rest on the inherent powers of government; whether derived in succession to the native authority from the grant of the Dewanny, or from those Statutes by which the general power of government or of ordering the revenues had been given or continued to the Company.

Statute law in 1834.

Thus from time to time the legislative powers of the Councils were developed; and in pursuance of those powers they enacted laws and regulations till 1834. Down to that date, which is the important epoch in the history of Indian legislation, there were five different bodies of Statute law in force in the empire. *First*, there was the whole body of English Statute law existing in 1726 so far as it was applicable, which was introduced by the Charter of George I., and which applied, at least, in the Presidency Towns. *Secondly*, all English Acts subsequent to that date which are expressly extended to any part of India. *Thirdly*, the Regulations of the Governor-General's Council, which commence with the Revised Code of 1793, containing forty-eight regulations, all passed on the same day (which embraced the results of

LECTURE IV.

twelve years' antecedent legislation), and were continued down to the year 1834. They only had force in the territories within the Presidency of Bengal. *Fourthly*, the Regulations of the Madras Council, which spread over the period of thirty-two years, *viz.* from 1802 to 1834, and were in force in the Presidency of Fort St. George. *Fifthly*, the Regulations of the Bombay Code, which began with the Revised Code of Mr. Mountstuart Elphinstone in 1827, comprising the results of twenty-eight years' previous legislation, and were also continued till 1834, having force and validity in the Presidency of Fort St. David.

Necessity for reform in the Legislature.

In 1833 the attention of Parliament was directed to three leading vices in the frame of Indian Government. The first was in the nature of the laws and regulations; the second was in the ill-defined authority and power from which these various laws and regulations emanated; and the third was the anomalous and sometimes conflicting Judicatures by which the laws were administered, or in other words the defects were in the laws themselves, in the authority for making them, and in the manner of executing them. The * Judges of the Supreme Court at Calcutta thus expressed themselves in reference to this subject:—"In this state of circumstances, no one can pronounce an opinion, or form a judgment, however sound, upon any disputed right of persons, respecting which doubt and confusion may not be raised by those who may choose to call it in question; for very few of the public or persons in office at home, not even the law officers, can be expected to have so comprehensive and clear a view of the Indian system, as to know readily and familiarly the bearings of each part of it on the rest. There are English Acts of Parliament specially provided for India, and others of which it is doubtful whether they apply to India wholly, or in part, or not at all. There is the English common law and

* See Hansard's "Parliamentary Debates" (1833), vol. xviii., p. 729.

LECTURE IV.

constitution, of which the application is, in many respects, still more obscure and perplexed; Mahomedan law and usage; Hindu law, usage, and scripture; Charters and Letters Patent of the Crown; Regulations of the Governments, some made declaredly under Acts of Parliament, particularly authorizing them, and others which are founded, as some say, on the general power of government entrusted to the Company by Parliament, and as others assert on their rights as successors of the old Native Government; some Regulations require registry in the Supreme Court; others do not; some have effect generally throughout India; others are peculiar to one Presidency or one town. There are commissions of the Governments, and Circular Orders from the Nizamut Adawlut and from the Dewanny Adawlut; treaties of the Crown; treaties of the Indian Government; besides inferences drawn at pleasure from the application of the *droit public* and the law of nations of Europe, to a state of circumstances which will justify almost any construction of it, or qualification of its force."

The Act of William the Fourth.

Accordingly in that year an Act * was passed "for effecting an arrangement with the East India Company and for the better government of Her Majesty's Indian territories till April 30th, 1854." It was enacted in the 43rd section "that the Governor-General in Council should have power to make laws and regulations for repealing, amending, or altering any laws or regulations whatever now in force or hereafter to be in force in the said territories or any part thereof; to make laws and regulations for all persons, whether British or Native, foreigners or others, and for all Courts of Justice, whether established by Her Majesty's Charters or otherwise, and the jurisdiction thereof and for all places and things whatsoever within and throughout the whole and every part of the said territories and for all servants of the said Company."

* 3 & 4 Wm. IV., c. 85.

LECTURE IV.

The exceptions to this sweeping power were that the Governor-General in Council should not have power to make any laws which should affect any of the provisions of this Act or of the Mutiny Acts, or of any Act thereafter to be passed in anywise affecting the Company, or the said territories, or the inhabitants thereof; nor should it have power to make any laws which should in any way affect any prerogative of the Crown, or the authority of Parliament, or the constitution or rights of the Company, or any part of the unwritten laws * or constitution of the United Kingdom of Great Britain and Ireland, "whereon may depend in any degree the allegiance of any person to the Crown of the United Kingdom, or the sovereignty or dominion of the Crown over any part of the said territories."

By a later Act, 16 & 17 Vict. c. 95, s. 26, no law was to be rendered invalid, only because it affected any prerogative of the Crown, provided the previous sanction of the Crown had been obtained.

The following provisions were made in the Act of William IV.:—

Provisions relative to legislation.

(1.) That the Governor-General in Council should forthwith repeal all laws which should be made by him, but be disallowed by the Court of Directors.

(2.) That all his laws should be of the same force and effect within the said territories as an Act of Parliament, and should be taken notice of by all Courts of Justice. Registration in any Court of Justice was declared unnecessary.

(3.) The Legislature could not, without the previous sanction of the Court of Directors, authorize any Court of Justice not established by Royal Charter to sentence to death any of His Majesty's natural-born subjects born in Europe, or the children of such subjects. Nor could it abolish any of the Courts of Justice established by Royal Charter.

* See *postea*, page 82, *note*.

An express reservation was made of the right of Parliament to continue to legislate for the Indian territories and their inhabitants; to control, supersede, or prevent all proceedings and acts whatsoever of the Governor-General in Council, and to repeal and alter at any time any law whatsoever made by him. And the better to enable Parliament to exercise such power, the laws of the new Legislature were directed to be laid before both Houses of Parliament in the same manner as those which had been previously made by the several Governments in India.

Indian Law Commissioners.

Some subsequent Sections * relate to the establishment of the Indian Law Commissioners.

Local Legislatures superseded.

No power was given in this Act to the Governors in Council of the different Presidencies to make laws, but they were empowered to propose drafts of new laws with the reasons for them to the Governor-General in Council; who was required to take the same into consideration, and to communicate his resolutions thereon to the Government which had proposed them.

Articles of War.

By Section 73, the power to make Articles of War for the Government of the Native officers and soldiers in the military service of the Company and for the administration of justice by Courts Martial, which had by the Act of 1813 been distributed over the three Legislatures, was now vested in the Governor-General in Council.

Conclusion.

Thus there was established in India one central legislative authority in place of the three Councils which had before existed. The new Council was armed with authority to pass Laws and Regulations for the whole of the British territories in India. It continued to exist with some changes and modifications till 1861, when it again gave way to the prevalent desire for local legislative Councils. During that time it passed a considerable number of Acts, some of general

* Sections 52, 53, 54, and 55.

LECTURE IV.

application throughout the empire, but the greater portion having a limited and partial operation. Local Legislatures had been tried and superseded by an Imperial Legislature, which in its turn was found inadequate to the political necessities of the country. An attempt was made to increase its usefulness and authority in 1853. But in 1861 a new system was introduced by which local Legislatures were re-established, not to supersede, but to work in harmony with, and to a certain extent in subordination to, the Legislative Council of the Viceroy. The Supreme Council, however, retains the power of making laws and regulations for the whole of India, as well over those portions which are subject to, as over those which are freed from a local legislative control. The changes which in 1853 were made in the constitution of the Council of 1834, and the character of the new legislative system which was established in 1861, will be described in the next Lecture.

LECTURE V.

THE LEGISLATIVE COUNCILS—(*Continued*).

Reform of the Council in 1853—Nature of the changes made—Effect thereof—The Legislatures of 1834 and 1853 compared—Advantages of the new system—Desire for local Legislatures—Despatch of Lord Canning—His proposal to establish local Legislatures—View of the English Government—The Indian Councils Act, 1861—The Governor-General's Council—Assent to laws—Legislative powers of the Council—Legislative power of the Governor-General—Local Legislatures at Madras and Bombay—Previous sanction of the Governor-General necessary to certain Bills—Power to the Governor-General in Council to establish other local Legislatures—Power of Legislatures so established—Local Legislatures in Bengal and North-West Punjab and British Burma—Act of 1861 amended in 1892—Character and functions of the Councils.

Reform of the Council in 1853.

THE Legislature established by the Act of 1834 lasted for twenty-seven years; but a considerable change was made in its character and constitution by an Act passed in 1853. The former Act was passed for a period of twenty years, and accordingly fresh legislation became necessary. Though the Council was continued upon the same footing in respect of its being the one legislative authority of India competent to enact laws for the whole of the British territories therein, the new * Act made so many alterations that the system was entirely changed. The principal alteration, which finally led to the re-establishment of local Legislatures, was the introduction of representative members from the sister Presidencies.

* 16 & 17 Vict., c. 95—An Act to provide for the government of India.

LECTURE V.

Nature of the changes made.

It was provided by the new Act passed in 1853 * that certain Legislative Councillors should be added to the existing Council; that no law made by the Council should have force or be promulgated until the same had been assented to by the Governor-General whether he had or had not been present in Council at the making thereof; and that no such law should be invalid by reason only that the same affected any prerogative of the Crown, provided the previous sanction of the Crown thereto had been obtained. It authorized Her Majesty to appoint a commission in England to consider the recommendations and reports of the Indian Law Commissioners.

Effect thereof.

The effect of the new Act was to enlarge the Council, when acting in its legislative capacity, by the addition of new members, called Legislative Members, of whom two were English Judges of the Calcutta Supreme Court, and the others were appointed severally by the local Governments. At the same time the fourth ordinary Councillor, who held under the former Act the corresponding office of Legislative Member, was made a member in the executive branch as well as in the legislative branch. Consequent upon these changes, discussion became oral instead of in writing; bills were referred to select committees instead of a single member; and legislative business was conducted in public instead of in secret. The system so introduced was considered by those who were well versed in it to be an infinite improvement upon the former system.

The Legislatures of 1834 and 1853 compared.

Under the former Act the sole power of making laws in India was vested in the Governor-General of India in Council. That body consisted of the Governor-General and four ordinary members of Council; the Commander-in-Chief, if appointed an extraordinary member of Council, also formed one of the body. Of the four ordinary members it

* 16 & 17 Vict., c. 95, s. 22.

was directed that three should be appointed from persons in the covenanted service of the East India Company, and the fourth from persons who had never been in the service. The duty of the fourth ordinary member was confined entirely to the subject of legislation. He had no power to sit and vote in the Executive Council, but only when meetings were held for the purpose of making laws. It was not necessary that he should be present to form a quorum even at those meetings, although he was particularly charged with the duties of legislation. He * was bound to give his whole time and attention to the work of legislation, but he had no pre-eminent control over it. He was charged with the task of giving shape and connexion to the several laws as they passed, with the labour of collecting local information, and with bringing his legal skill to the assistance of the Council.

By the Act of 1853 the duties which under the former Act had rested principally on the fourth ordinary member of Council were performed by many. The Governor of each Presidency and the Lieutenant-Governor of each Lieutenant-Governorship were empowered to appoint a Legislative Councillor. The Legislative Councillors so appointed were members of the service of a certain standing, and therefore of knowledge and experience.

Advantages of the new system.

Such a system had many advantages over that which preceded it, even while the Indian Law Commission was in full operation; for the Legislative Councillors had the power which the Law Commissioners had not of proposing any law which they considered necessary or beneficial, of opposing any law which they deemed unnecessary or injurious, of supporting their opinion by argument in Council, and of voting on every subject which came under discussion. The Legislative Council was not diminished in other respects: for every member of the Executive Council, including the fourth

* Consult Minute of Mr. Peacock, dated 3rd November, 1859.

LECTURE V.

member who obtained the power to sit and vote at all meetings, was also a member of the Legislative Council; it was simply increased by members of practical experience. In addition to the Legislative Councillor, the Chief Justice of Bengal and one of the Puisne Judges of the Supreme Court selected by the Governor-General were also members; and six members in addition to the Governor-General or the Vice-President or Chairman were necessary to form a quorum, and the presence of one of the Judges or of the fourth ordinary member was rendered essential.

Desire for local Legislatures.

Notwithstanding the improvements which it was considered on all hands that the Act of 1853 had introduced, it became necessary to re-consider the whole subject of the establishment and exercise of legislative authority. Madras and Bombay complained of the enormous preponderance of authority which Bengal through her Council acquired over the sister Presidencies. The wide extent of dominion subject to the legislation of the Council rendered it impossible that all questions could be settled by the light of adequate information and experience. And the internal governance of the Council itself was such that it was rapidly assuming the character, contrary to the intentions of Parliament, of a representative and debating society assembled for the purposes of inquiry into and redress of grievances.

Despatch of Lord Canning.

Lord Canning, in a despatch dated the 9th December, 1859, pointed out what he considered to be the chief faults of the Legislature as it then existed. In the first place it was invested with forms and modes of procedure closely imitating those of the House of Commons. There were 136 standing orders to regulate the proceedings of a dozen gentlemen assembled in Council, which led to delay and confusion. The assumption of the procedure of the House of Commons caused the impression, contrary to the intentions of Government, that reports and returns should be ordered by the

Council from the local administrations, that long debates should be held on questions of public interest, and that measures should be introduced independently of the Executive Government.

Lord Canning also expressed his opinion with reference to the constitution of the Council that although a return to the system which existed before 1853 was impossible, it well deserved consideration whether a partial return to the still earlier system which prevailed before 1834 was not advisable. "There is no doubt," he says, "that the introduction of a single member from each local Government has been a great advantage. But although an improvement has been thus made in the system antecedent to 1853, I do not think it has been carried far enough. I do not think that the principle of representing the local Governments having been once admitted, the Governments of Madras and Bombay can be reasonably expected to be satisfied with the share which they at present have in any legislation directly concerning their own Presidencies, and I believe that by giving them a much larger share in it, careful local measures may be facilitated and expedited, without leading to any interference with measures of a general character, or with the authority and responsibilities of the Governor-General in Council."

His proposal to establish local Legislatures.

The Governor-General, after discussing and condemning an alternative suggestion to increase in the existing Council the number of members drawn from the two subordinate Presidencies, proposed that the Council should be broken up into three distinct Councils at Calcutta, Madras, and Bombay.

He proposed not merely that the Governors of Madras and Bombay should each have a Legislative Council, but that Bengal and the North-West Provinces and the Punjab should each have its separate Legislature. He also said that two things were essential in forming a body of advisers to the Governor-General in legislative matters. One that it

Lecture V.

should be capable of being assembled for business in other places than Calcutta; and the other that it should so conduct its business as that the opinions and votes of Natives not skilled in the English language could be taken. He proposed that all measures of local administration not affecting the revenue should fall within the competency of the local Councils; but that if the matter affected the revenue, the sanction of the Governor-General in Council should be first obtained to the introduction of a bill upon the subject. The making of laws for those provinces which have no Legislative Councils, that is for non-regulation Provinces, should be vested in the Legislative Council of the Governor-General.

The events which immediately led to the passing of the Indian Councils Act, 1861, were the differences which arose between the Supreme Government and the Government of Madras on the Income Tax Bill; the doubts which had been raised as to the validity of laws introduced into non-regulation Provinces without enactment by the Legislative Council; and the address of the Legislative Council for the communication to it of certain correspondence between the Secretary of State and the Supreme Government of India.

View of the English Government.

Sir Charles Wood, in introducing the Bill into the House of Commons, recapitulated* the objections to the existing institution, which appeared to be quite as strongly felt by the Home authorities as by the Government in India. He complained that, quite contrary to what was intended, the Council had become a sort of debating society or petty parliament. He quoted Sir Lawrence Peel's criticism upon its proceedings, that it "has no jurisdiction in the nature of that of a grand inquest of the nation. Its functions are purely legislative, and are limited even in that respect. It is not an Anglo-Indian House of Commons for the redress of grievances, to refuse supplies, and so forth."

* See Hansard's "Parliamentary Debates," vol. clxiii., p. 639.

The view which was taken by the English Government of the changes which had become necessary was thus explained: "I propose," said the Secretary of State, "that when the Council meets for the purpose of making laws, the Governor-General should summon, in addition to the * ordinary members of the Council, not less than six nor more than twelve additional members, of whom one-half at least shall not hold office under the Government. These additional members may be either Europeans, persons of European extraction, or Natives. Lord Canning strongly recommends that the Council should hold its meetings in different parts of India for the purpose of obtaining at times the assistance of those Native chiefs and nobles whose attendance at Calcutta would be impossible, or irksome to themselves. I do not propose that the Judges *ex officio* shall have seats in the Legislature; but I do not preclude the Governor-General from summoning one of their number if he chooses. The Council of the Governor-General, with these additional members, will have power to pass laws and regulations affecting the whole of India, and will have a supreme and concurrent power with the minor legislative bodies which I propose to establish in the Presidencies and other parts of India."

And with respect to giving the power of making laws to the Governors and Councils of other Presidencies, he says, "Lord Canning strongly feels that although great benefits have resulted from the introduction of members into his Council who possess a knowledge of localities, the interest of which differs widely in different parts of the country; yet the change has not been sufficient in the first place to overcome the feeling which the other Presidencies entertain against being overridden, as they call it, by the Bengal Council; or, on the other hand, to overcome the disadvantages of having a

* These were increased to five and afterwards to six. See 24 & 25 Vict. c. 67, s. 3; 32 & 33 Vict. c. 97, s. 8; 37 & 38 Vict. c. 91.

LECTURE V.

body legislating for these Presidencies without acquaintance with local wants and necessities. This must obviously be possessed to a much greater extent by those residing on the spot. And, therefore, I propose to restore, I may say to the Presidencies of Madras and Bombay, the power of passing laws and enactments on local subjects within their own territories; and that the Governor of the Presidency, in the same manner as the Governor-General, when his Council meets to make laws, shall summon a certain number of additional members, to be as before, either European or Native, and one-half of whom at least shall not be office-holders."

The Indian Councils Act, 1861.

Thus the "Indian Councils Act, 1861," * was passed in order to consolidate and amend former Acts of Parliament respecting the constitution and functions of the Council of the Governor-General, and to give power to the Governors in Council in Madras and Bombay to make laws for the government of those Presidencies, and to enable the like legislative authority to be constituted in other parts of Her Majesty's Indian dominions.

The Governor-General's Council.

The Governor-General in Council is authorized to appoint the times and places of meeting † of his Legislative Council, and under certain restrictions to make rules for the conduct of its business. The Legislative Council has no power to transact any business other than the consideration and enactment of measures introduced into the Council for the purpose of such enactment. The previous sanction of the Governor-General is necessary before any measure can be introduced into Council affecting (1) the public debt or public revenue of India, or by which any charge can be imposed on such revenue; (2) the religion or religious rites and usages of any class of Her Majesty's subjects in India; (3) the discipline or maintenance of any part of Her Majesty's military or naval

* 24 & 25 Vict. c. 67.

† See also 33 Vict. c. 3, s. 3.

forces; (4) the relation of the Government with foreign princes or states.

Assent to laws.

The assent of the Governor-General to any law is necessary to its validity, whether or not he has been present in Council at the making thereof. The Governor-General can withhold his assent absolutely, or may reserve the same for the pleasure of Her Majesty thereon; whose assent in that case is necessary, and will be signified through the Secretary of State for India in Council. The Crown also has power to disallow any law which has been assented to by the Governor-General. In that case the law so disallowed will be made void and annulled from the date on which the Governor-General shall proclaim or signify to his Council that it has been disallowed.

Legislative powers of the Council.

The legislative powers of the Council extend (1) to repeal, amend or alter any laws or regulations in force in the British territories in India; (2) to make laws for all persons, whether British or Native, foreigners or others, and for all Courts of Justice, and for all places and things within those territories; (3) for all British subjects, whether or not in the service of the Government of India, within the dominions of princes and states in alliance with Her Majesty;* (4) for all Native Indian subjects beyond the Indian territories.† But it was expressly declared that that legislative authority should not extend to repeal or in any way affect any provisions of any Act of Parliament passed at any time after the year 1860 which in anywise affects Her Majesty's Indian territories or the inhabitants thereof. Nor does it extend to pass any law which may affect the authority of Parliament, or the constitution and rights of the East India Company, or any part of the unwritten laws or constitution of the United Kingdom of Great Britain and Ireland whereon may depend in any degree the allegiance of any person to the Crown of the

* See 28 & 29 Vict. c. 17.

† See 32 & 33 Vict. c. 98.

LECTURE V. United Kingdom, or the sovereignty or dominion of the Crown over any part of the said territories.*

* The Indian Councils Act contains the same expressions as those used in the earlier Act of William the Fourth (section 43). Their meaning was the subject of discussion in the case of *Ameer Khan*, and I append the following passage from the judgment of Mr. Justice Norman in that case; See 6 Bengal Law Reports, p. 450:—

"In order to see what is meant by the words 'unwritten laws or constitution whereon may depend in any degree the allegiance of any person,' it is necessary to consider first what allegiance is. It is the true and faithful obedience of the subject to the sovereign. Everyone born within the dominions of the king of England, or in the colonies or dependencies, being under the protection therefore according to our common law, owes allegiance to the king. Every British subject is born a debtor by the fealty and allegiance which he owes his sovereign and the State, a creditor by the benefit and protection of the king, the laws, and the constitution. 'Allegiance,' says Sir William Blackstone (*a*), 'is the tie which binds the subject to the king in return for that protection which the king affords to the subject.' Foremost amongst the privileges assured to the subject by the protection of the sovereign is liberty and security of the person. The Crown cannot derogate from those rights. Bracton tells us that 'the king is under the law, for the law makes the king.' The king cannot interfere with the liberty of the subject, nor deprive him of any of his rights. How absolute soever the sovereigns of other nations may be, the king of England cannot take up or detain the meanest subject at his mere will and pleasure.

"I will proceed to consider what are the 'unwritten laws and constitution' of the United Kingdom which are alluded to in the section (*b*). It is well known that the provisions of the Great Charter and the Petition of Right are for the most part declarations of what the existing law was, not enactments of any new law. They set forth and assert the right of the subject, according to what was assumed to be the ancient unwritten laws and constitution of the realm. * * *

"Now if it be true that allegiance and protection are reciprocally due from the subject and the sovereign, it is evident that the strict observance of the laws which provide for such liberty and security ensures the faithful and loving allegiance of subjects. * * * *

"On the faithful observance by the sovereign of the unwritten laws and constitution of the United Kingdom, as contained in the Great Charter and other Acts which I have mentioned, depend in no small

(*a*) 2 Stephen's Blackstone, p. 413.
(*b*) 3 & 4 Wm. IV. c. 85, s. 43.

Lecture V.

And in particular the Council has no authority to repeal or affect by their legislation any of the provisions which, at the time of the passing of the Indian Councils Act, remained in force of the Acts * noted below.

Nor can it affect any Act enabling the Secretary of State in Council to raise money in the United Kingdom for the Government of India, nor any Act for punishing mutiny and desertion in Her Majesty's Army or in Her Majesty's Indian forces respectively.†

It was provided that no law made by the Governor-General in Council shall be deemed invalid by reason only that it affected the prerogative of the Crown. And it was further enacted that the laws and regulations which had been previously made in respect of any non-regulation province should not be deemed ‡ invalid, notwithstanding any doubts which might be entertained whether they had been made in due conformity with or in pursuance of any valid legislative authority.

Legislative power of the Governor-General.

In case of emergency the Governor-General is vested with the authority of his Legislative Council to make and promulgate from time to time ordinances ‡ for the peace and good government of the British territories in India or any part thereof. An ordinance, however, so made would

degree the allegiance of the subjects. It would be a startling thing to find that they could be taken away by an Act of the subordinate Legislature. It would be a strange thing indeed if a great popular assembly, like the Parliament of England, had put into the power of a Legislature which has not, and in the nature of things cannot have any representative character, the power of abrogating or tampering with such fundamental laws."

* 3 & 4 Will. IV. c. 85 (but see 32 & 33 Vict. c. 98, s. 3); 16 & 17 Vict. c. 95, 17 & 18 Vict. c. 77; 21 & 22 Vict. c. 106, entitled "an Act for the better government of India," and 22 & 23 Vict. c. 41, passed to amend the same.

† This is subject to the provisions contained in 3 & 4 Will. IV. c. 85, s. 73, respecting the Indian Articles of War.

‡ See *note* at the end of this Lecture, page 88.

LECTURE V.

only have validity for the space of six months from its promulgation, and might be earlier disallowed by Her Majesty, or controlled or superseded by a law passed by the Legislative Council.

Local Legislatures at Madras and Bombay.

The same Act vested in the Governors of Madras and Bombay power to nominate, in addition to the ordinary members of their Councils, certain persons who should be entitled to sit and vote at meetings thereof held for the purpose of making laws. The power to legislate was vested in the Governor in Council, who was authorized to appoint times and places for its meeting, and to make rules for the conduct of its business which, with his assent, might be subsequently amended at meetings of the Council. The assent of the Governor was necessary to the validity of a law, whether or not he was present at the meeting at which it was made. The further assent of the Governor-General was necessary to the validity of such law; in case of such assent being withheld, the Governor-General must signify to the Governor in writing his reason for withholding it. His assent gives validity to the law, subject nevertheless to its disallowance by Her Majesty through the Secretary of State for India in Council.

The legislative authority, so created in each of the two subordinate Presidencies, extends to repeal and amend any laws made prior to the coming into operation of the Indian Councils Act by any authority in India, so far as they affect such Presidency, but does not extend to legislate, so as in any way to affect the provisions of any Act of Parliament then or thereafter to be enforced in such Presidency.*

Previous sanction of the Governor-General necessary to certain bills.

The previous sanction of the Governor-General is necessary before either of such Councils can take into consideration any law for any of these purposes: (1), affecting the public debt

* For an extension of the power of local Legislatures as regards European British subjects, see 34 & 35 Vict. c. 34.

of India, or the custom duties, or any other tax or duty then in force, and imposed by the authority or the Government of India for the general purposes of such government; (2), regulating any of the current coin or the issue of any bills, notes, or other paper currency; (3), regulating the conveyance by the Post Office, or messages by the Electric Telegraph within the Presidency; (4), altering in any way the Penal Code of India as established by Act XLV. of 1860; (5), affecting the religion or religious rites and usages of any class of Her Majesty's subjects in India; (6), affecting the discipline or maintenance of any part of her Majesty's Military or Naval Forces; (7), regulating patents or copyright; (8), affecting the relations of the Government with foreign princes or states.

It was further provided that no law which shall have been made by any such Governor in Council, and assented to by the Governor-General, shall be deemed invalid only by reason of its relating to any of the purposes comprised in the above list.

Power to the Governor-General in Council to establish other local Legislatures.

No Local Legislatures were established in India by the Act, except those at Madras and Bombay. But the Governor-General in Council was empowered to extend by proclamation such provisions of the Act as related to the legislative authority in those two Presidencies, to the Bengal division of the Presidency of Fort William; and at his discretion to extend those provisions to the North-West Provinces and the Punjab. He was further empowered by proclamation to constitute from time to time new Provinces for the purposes of the Act to which the like provisions should be applicable, and to fix or alter the limits of any Presidency or Province for the purposes of the Act.

Powers of Legislatures so established.

Every Lieutenant-Governor in Council thus constituted is empowered to make laws for the peace and good government of his province or territory. All the provisions contained in the Act which limited the legislative power of the Governors in Council of the two subordinate Presidencies, and which

LECTURE V.

related to the Governor-General's power to declare or withhold his assent to laws made in pursuance of such authority, and which related to the power of Her Majesty to disallow the same, were declared to apply to any laws or regulations which might be made by a Lieutenant-Governor in Council.

The previous assent of the Crown was rendered necessary to give validity to any of the foregoing proclamations which the Governor-General was authorized to make.

The local Legislatures have no power to control or affect by their acts the jurisdiction or procedure of the High Courts. The power of doing so rests with Parliament and the Legislative Council of the Governor-General.*

Local Legislatures in Bengal and North-West Punjab and British Burma.

The despatch of Sir C. Wood, which accompanied the Act, directed the Governor-General at once to extend the necessary provisions of the Act to the Bengal Division of the Presidency of Fort William.† Accordingly, a proclamation was issued constituting the Bengal Legislative Council on the 17th January, 1862. On the 26th November, 1886, another proclamation was issued constituting a legislative council for the North-West Provinces and Oudh. And on the 9th April, 1897, a third proclamation was issued constituting a legislative council for the territories known as the Punjab. In 1898, a similar council was established for British Burma.

The local Legislatures thus established differ from those which existed before the Act of William the Fourth in this important respect, that in former times the regulations of the local Legislatures were complete, and came into operation without reference to the Governor-General; while under the Indian Councils Act,‡ the local Governor is bound to transmit an authenticated copy of any law to which he has assented to

* See the Indian High Courts Act, 24 & 25 Vict. c. 104, s. 9, and the 37th Section of the Bengal Charter and corresponding sections in the other Charters.

† Despatch dated 9th August, 1861.

‡ See Section 40.

the Governor-General. No local law has any validity till the Governor-General has assented thereto, and such assent shall have been signified by him to, and published by, the Governor. If the assent is withheld, the Governor-General must signify his reason in writing for so doing.

The Governor-General, therefore, is at the head of all the legislative authority exercised in British India. Besides the legislative authority created by the Indian Councils Act, 1861, the Governor-General in Council is specially empowered by a later Act to pass certain local laws otherwise than at a meeting of his Legislative Council.* This power has been frequently used and many Regulations so made are in force in Upper Burma (originally King Thebaw's dominions), Ajmere, Coorg, Assam and other places.

Act of 1861 amended in 1892.

†An Act passed in 1892 amended the Indian Councils Act of 1861. Its chief object was to increase the number of councillors and to authorize discussion of the financial statement of the Government and the asking of questions. The powers of the Provincial Legislatures were extended to repealing and amending laws made by any other authority than the local legislature concerned, either before or after the passing of the new Act.

Character and function of the Councils.

The character of these Legislative Councils is simply this, that they are committees for the purpose of making laws, committees by means of which the Executive Government obtains advice and assistance in their legislation, and the public derive the advantage of full publicity being ensured at every stage of the law-making process. Although the Government enacts the laws through its Council, private legislation being unknown, yet the public has a right to make itself heard and the Executive is bound to defend its legislation. And when the laws are once made the Executive is as much

* See 33 Vict. c. 3.
† 55 & 56 Vict. c. 92.

LECTURE V. bound by them as the public, and the duty of enforcing them belongs to the Courts of Justice. Such laws are in reality the orders of Government, but they are made in a manner which ensures publicity and discussion, are enforced by the Courts and not by the Executive, cannot be changed but by the same deliberate and public process as that by which they were made, and can be enforced against the Executive or in favour of individuals wherever occasion requires.

The Councils are not deliberative bodies with respect to any subject but that of the immediate legislation or financial policy before them. They cannot inquire into grievances, call for information, or examine the conduct of the Executive. The acts of administration cannot be impugned, nor can they be properly defended in such assemblies, except with reference to the particular measure under discussion.

NOTE.—Up to the passing of the Indian Councils Act, 1861, the Executive Government legislated, by means of Circulars and Orders and Rules issued to their officers, for the Non-Regulation Provinces. The Act gave Legislative force to all the miscellaneous and ill-digested rules which had thus originated. The Non-Regulation Provinces are therefore subject to a body of law dissimilar in its origin and character from that of any other civilized country.

No Legislative force belongs to any rules and orders which have been issued by the Executive Government since that Act. The Governor-General's Council possesses the sole Legislative authority for the Non-Regulation Provinces.

With regard to the power of the Governor-General to make ordinances, referred to in page 83 of the text, it was first exercised by Lord Mayo, once in 1869 for the purpose of imposing an additional half per cent. of Income Tax, and afterwards in the same year to exclude a disturbed portion of territory on the frontiers of the Punjab from the jurisdiction of the Civil Courts.*

* See Broughton's State of the Law in the Non-Regulation Provinces, p. 16.

LECTURE VI.

LATER HISTORY: THE PRESIDENCY TOWN SYSTEM.

The Presidency Town system—Duration of the Supreme Court at Calcutta—Inconveniences of the double system—Extension of criminal jurisdiction—Of the Admiralty jurisdiction—Gaol Deliveries—Jurisdiction extended over the Province of Benares—Madras and Bombay—Recorders' Courts established in 1797—Supreme Court at Madras—Supreme Court at Bombay—Dissensions at Bombay—Inferior judicial authorities—Courts of Requests—Small Cause Courts—Justices of the Peace—Subject to the control of the Supreme Court—Appointment of Justices of the Peace—Their jurisdiction and Powers—Presidency Town Magistrates—Coroners—Rival judicial institutions—Tendency to amalgamation—Conclusion.

The Presidency Town system.

I NOW pass on to the history of the judicial institutions established in India previous to the introduction of the High Courts. Of these institutions several had been established by the Crown and Parliament before the acquisition of territorial sovereign power. Others were at a later period substituted for them by the same authority. Although the later Courts so established had some jurisdiction in the Provinces, yet they were originally intended for the benefit of the Company's factories, and subsequently for the Presidency Towns; and their retention served to maintain the separation between the Presidency Towns and the Mofussil. Notwithstanding their partial jurisdiction in the Mofussil, I have ventured to collect these institutions under the head of the Presidency Town system, including all which were established by the Crown or Parliament, and which were not vested with or did not exercise a general jurisdiction in the Provinces.

LECTURE VI.

Duration of the Supreme Court at Calcutta.

Foremost amongst these institutions came the Supreme Court at Calcutta, which, as it was finally established under the Act of 1781, continued to exist for a period of upwards of eighty years and was presided over by a long series of eminent Judges. In 1861 an Act * was passed which led in the next year to the abolition of a tribunal, which began in discredit and with general reprobation, but finally obtained a lasting hold on the respect and confidence alike of Natives and Europeans. Under the Act of 1861, Royal Charters were issued establishing the existing High Courts, and from the date of the new Courts coming into existence, *viz.* in July, 1862, the Supreme Court ceased to exist.

Inconveniences of the double system.

The history of the Court in Calcutta in the intermediate space of time was not marked by any of the dissensions and violent contests which preceded that period. But nevertheless, many inconveniences remained and were inseparable from the double system of judicial administration which prevailed. The Company's Courts had no jurisdiction for a long time, civil or criminal, over British-born subjects. The Crown Courts could harass but could not control the Courts of the Company with which they had occasionally concurrent jurisdiction, and had but little authority over the general course of justice. There was, as Chief Justice Sir C. Grey pointed out,† an utter want of connection between the Supreme Court and the Provincial Courts and the two sorts of legal process which were employed in them. And the exercise of the powers of the one system was viewed with jealousy by those who were connected with the other; every Court in India being further liable to be perplexed by the obligation which more or less was imposed upon all, of administering three or four different sorts of law to as many classes of persons. Nevertheless the two systems were

* 24 & 25 Vict. c. 104.

† Sir C. E. Grey's Minute, p. 1154.

maintained; and the jurisdiction of the Supreme Court was from time to time extended by various Acts of Parliament to which I shall now refer.

Extension of criminal jurisdiction.

With regard to criminal jurisdiction an Act * of Parliament was passed in 1784, the effect of which was to vest the Supreme Court with jurisdiction to try all criminal offences committed by any of His Majesty's subjects in the territories of any Native Prince or State, or against their persons or properties, or the persons or properties of any of their subjects or people, in the same manner as if the same had been committed within the territories directly subject to the British Government in India. Two years later another † Act of Parliament was passed, whereby all servants of the East India Company and all His Majesty's subjects resident in India were made subject to the Courts of Oyer and Terminer and Gaol Delivery for all criminal offences committed in any part of Asia, Africa, and America, beyond the Cape of Good Hope and the Straits of Magellan, within the limits of the Company's trade.

By the same Act ‡ jurisdiction, as well civil as criminal, was given to the Governor's Council and Mayor's Court at Madras over all British subjects residing in the territories of the East India Company on the Coast of Coromandel, or in any other part of the Carnatic or in the Northern Circars or within the territories of the Soubah of the Deccan, the Nabob of Arcot, or the Rajah of Tanjore.

Of the Admiralty jurisdiction.

With regard to the Admiralty jurisdiction doubts arose how far in criminal matters it was limited by the original Charter to offences committed on the coast of Bengal, Behar, and Orissa within the ebbing and flowing of the sea at high water mark. An Act of Parliament § accordingly extended

* 24 Geo. III. c. 25, s. 44.

† 26 Geo. III. c. 57, s. 29.

‡ Section 30.

§ 33 Geo. III. c. 52, s. 156.

LECTURE VI.

the power and authority of the Court to the high seas so as to give a full jurisdiction over all offences committed thereon to be exercised according to the laws and customs of the Admiralty of England. Seven years later* the Crown was empowered to appoint all or any of the Judges of the Supreme Court at Fort William (or of either of the similar Courts at Madras and Bombay) either alone or jointly with others to be Commissioners for the trial and adjudication of prize causes and other maritime questions arising in India. And a further doubt having arisen whether the Admiralty jurisdiction of the Courts of Calcutta, Madras, and Bombay extended to any persons but those who were amenable to their ordinary jurisdiction, it was enacted† that they might take cognizance of all crimes perpetrated on the high seas by any person or persons whatsoever in as full and ample a manner as any other Court of Admiralty Jurisdiction established by His Majesty's authority in any colony or settlement whatsoever belonging to the Crown of the United Kingdom.

Gaol Deliveries.

It was also enacted,‡ in order to prevent any delay of justice or the unnecessary detention of persons charged with offences, that all His Majesty's Courts exercising criminal jurisdiction within the three Presidencies of the Company should, four times at the least in every year, hold their sessions for the purpose of taking cognizance of all matters relating to pleas of the Crown.

Jurisdiction over the Province of Benares.

Some time after the establishment of the Supreme Court at Calcutta the province or district of Benares was ceded to the Company and was annexed to the Presidency of Fort William. Parliament thereupon enacted that that province as well as all other provinces or districts which might thereafter at any time be annexed should, with their subordinate

* 39 & 40 Geo. III. c. 79, s. 25.

† 53 Geo. III. c. 155, s. 110.

‡ *Ibid.* sec. 102.

factories, be subject to the jurisdiction of the Court.* As regards the Benares district the Act took effect from the first of March, 1801.

LECTURE VI.

The powers of the Supreme Court were thus gradually extended within the limits marked out by the Act of 1781. It had five jurisdictions, *viz.* civil, criminal, equity, ecclesiastical, and Admiralty. An appeal lay to the Privy Council in all suits when the amount in dispute was of the value of Rs. 10,000.

Madras and Bombay.

In the Presidencies of Madras and Bombay the experiment of establishing a Supreme Court was not made for some time; and apparently it was in contemplation to abstain altogether from it.

Recorders' Courts established in 1797.

The Mayors' Courts, which were established at Madras and Bombay in 1753, existed till the year 1797, nearly a quarter of a century longer than the similar tribunal in Calcutta. Even in that year, when they were abolished, Parliament did not establish Supreme Courts in their stead. They were replaced by Recorders' Courts.† These consisted of the Mayor, three Aldermen, and a Recorder, being in fact the old Mayors' Courts, with the addition of a Recorder to each Court, who was to be appointed by the Crown. They had civil, criminal, ecclesiastical, and Admiralty jurisdiction. They had power to try all suits which by authority of Parliament could be tried in the Mayors' Courts. Their jurisdiction extended over British subjects resident within the British territories subject to the Governments of Madras and Bombay respectively, or within the territories of Native Princes in alliance with these Governments.

Restrictions corresponding to those imposed by Parliament in 1781 on the jurisdiction of the Supreme Court of Calcutta were made applicable to these Recorders' Courts.

Supreme

The new Courts did not last long. That at Madras existed

* 39 & 40 Geo. III. c. 79, s. 20.

† 37 Geo. III. c. 142.

LECTURE VI.

Court at Madras.

for two years and was then abolished,* a Supreme Court being established in its stead. The powers vested in the Recorder's Court were transferred to the new Supreme Court, which was also directed to have the like jurisdiction and to be subject to the same restrictions as the Supreme Court of Judicature at Fort William at Bengal. This new Charter was granted in December, 1801.

Supreme Court at Bombay.

The Recorder's Court at Bombay existed till 1823, when a Supreme Court of Judicature was established in its stead, and was invested with the same powers and authorities as the Supreme Court of Calcutta, with a similar jurisdiction and subject to the same limitations, restrictions, and control.

The Charter † of the Bombay Court appears to have been slightly different from the other two Charters. The Supreme Court in that Presidency was prohibited from interfering in any matter concerning the revenue, even within the town of Bombay. Natives also were exempted (and this provision appears in the Madras Charter also) from appearing therein, unless the circumstances were altogether such that they might have been compelled to appear in the same manner in a Native Court. In crimes maritime the Bombay Court's jurisdiction was restricted to such persons as would have been amenable to it in its ordinary jurisdiction.

Dissensions at Bombay.

The constitution of the Supreme Court at Bombay was followed shortly afterwards by disputes between the Court and the local Government similar in character (but on a smaller scale) to those which before 1781 had produced so much commotion in Bengal. The Judges, claiming the powers of the Court of King's Bench, issued writs of *Habeas Corpus*, one ‡ to bring a Native boy from Poona to Bombay, and another to compel a gaoler to produce a prisoner

* 39 & 40 Geo. III. c. 79.

† Morley's Digest, p. 20.

‡ *In re Justices of the Supreme Courts*, Knapp's Privy Council Reports, Vol. I., p. 1; and see case of *Moro Ragonath*, Asiatic Journal for April, 1829, and Mill's History of India, Vol. IX., p. 196.

detained under an order of one of the Company's Judges. The execution of the first was resisted by the Magistrate of Poona with the sanction of Government, because the affidavits on which it was granted were said to be false, and because neither Poona, nor the boy detained, nor the person detaining were subject to the jurisdiction of the Court. The other was resisted on the ground that the Supreme Court had no power to discharge persons imprisoned under the authority of a Native Court.

The proceedings came before the Privy Council on the petition of the sole surviving Judge who had issued the writs. The Privy Council decided that they had been improperly issued; that the Supreme Court at Bombay had no power to issue a writ of *Habeas Corpus*, except when directed either to a person resident within those local limits wherein such Court had a general jurisdiction, or to a person out of such local limits who was personally subject to its civil and criminal jurisdiction. They also held that the Court had no power to issue a writ of *Habeas Corpus* to the gaoler or officer of a Native Court as such officer, the Court having no power to discharge persons imprisoned under the authority of a Native Court.

Inferior judicial authorities.

The Supreme Courts were the chief tribunals which owed their authority exclusively to the English Parliament and Crown. There were, however, other judicial authorities, derived from the same source, which long existed in India (some of them not yet abolished), and which were originally established in days before the Company had obtained sovereign power and when they had merely to govern their own servants and those resident under their immediate protection.

Courts of Requests.

Courts of Requests, for instance, were established by the Charter of 1753, which renewed the Mayors' Courts in the three Presidency Towns. They were empowered to determine suits when the debt, duty, or matter in dispute did not

LECTURE VI.

exceed five pagodas, *i.e.* twenty rupees. In 1797* their jurisdiction was extended, the pecuniary limit being then fixed at eighty rupees. Two years later another Act † was passed which gave certain powers to the Governments of Bengal and Madras, under which Commissioners were established for the recovery of small debts, and their jurisdiction gradually extended up to 400 Sicca rupees.

Doubts arose as to the powers of the Calcutta Commissioners, and Act XII. of 1848 was passed better to define their jurisdiction. The Courts of Requests were originally made subject to the order and control of the Supreme Courts in the same manner as the inferior Courts in England are by law subject to the order and control of the Court of Queen's Bench.

Small Cause Courts.

These Courts of Requests were in 1850 superseded by the establishment of Small Cause Courts in the Presidency Towns. The jurisdiction of these new tribunals was subsequently extended and similar tribunals were also established in the Mofussil.

The Small Cause Courts, the Insolvent Courts, and the Vice-Admiralty Courts continue to exist at the present day and will be more conveniently described when I come to the subject of the existing judicial system.

Justices of the Peace.

The next judicial officers, who formed part of the Crown or Parliamentary system introduced into India, were the Justices of the Peace. They were first established at Madras, Bombay, and Calcutta by the Charter of George I. in 1726, which appointed the Governor and Councils of these places to be Justices of the Peace, with power to hold Quarter Sessions.

This was at a time when the only object was to introduce a purely English system for the benefit of English and other servants of the Company. The Regulating Act ‡ made the

* 37 Geo. III. c. 142, s. 30.
† 39 & 40 Geo. III. s. 17.
‡ 13 Geo. III. c. 63, s. 38.

Governor-General in Council and Judges of the Supreme Court Justices of the Peace for the settlement of Fort William and the settlements and factories subordinate thereto. The Governor-General and Council were directed to hold quarter sessions within the settlement of Fort William; such quarter sessions to be a Court of Record.

Subject to the control of the Supreme Court.

The Supreme Court Charter authorized the new Court to control the Court of Quarter Sessions and the Justices, exercising the same supervision and control over them as the Court of Queen's Bench exercises over the inferior Courts and Magistrates. It also empowered the Court to issue to them writs of *mandamus, certiorari, procedendo,* and *error*. The Judges of the Court were also appointed Justices of the Peace in the Lower Provinces of Bengal, with such jurisdiction and authority as Justices of the Queen's Bench have within England by the common law thereof.

Appointment of Justices of the Peace.

Originally the only Justices of the Peace in India were the Governors and Councils of the three Presidencies, and the Judges of the Calcutta Supreme Court. Subsequently, when Supreme Courts were established at Madras and Bombay, the Judges of those Courts were also made Justices of the Peace for their respective Presidencies; and the Courts were vested with the same authority as the Calcutta Supreme Court over the proceedings of the Justices.

In 1793 * an Act of Parliament empowered the Governor-General in Council to appoint Justices of the Peace from the covenanted servants of the Company, or other British inhabitants, to act within and for the three Presidencies and the places thereto subordinate respectively by commissions to be issued out of the Calcutta Supreme Court, on the warrant of the Governor-General in Council.

Justices so appointed were not to sit in any Court of Oyer and Terminer and Gaol Delivery, unless called upon by the Judges

* 33 Geo. III. c. 52, s. 151.

LECTURE VI.

of the Supreme Court and specially authorized by order in Council. All proceedings before Justices * of the Peace were removable by *certiorari* into the Court of Oyer and Terminer.

In 1807 † the Governors and Councils of Madras and Bombay were authorized to act as Justices of the Peace for those towns respectively, and to hold quarter sessions. They were also empowered to issue commissions under the seals of the Courts appointing British subjects to be Justices of the Peace in the provinces.

In 1832 ‡ the Governments of the three Presidencies were respectively empowered to appoint in the name of the King's Majesty, any persons resident within the territories of the Company, and not being subjects of any foreign State, to act within and for the three Presidency Towns respectively as Justices of the Peace.

Their jurisdiction and powers.

The Governments of the three § Presidencies, under the authority of Parliament, enacted from time to time various regulations authorizing and empowering Justices of the Peace to take cognizance of and punish certain offences.

Several Acts ‖ were passed by the Imperial Legislative Council to regulate the jurisdiction and powers of Justices of the Peace. Their jurisdiction extended over the whole Presidency for which they were appointed. The classes subject to them ¶ were—

(1.) All persons whatever, whether British or Native subjects, in respect of offences committed within the limits of the ordinary jurisdiction of the Supreme Courts.

(2.) All British subjects, resident in any part of the

* 47 Geo. III. c. 68, ss. 2, 4.

† See 153rd section of the same Act.

‡ 2 & 3 Wm. IV. c. 117.

§ See Morley's Administration of Justice, p. 36.

‖ See Act IV. of 1835, Act I. of 1837, Act XXXII. of 1838, Act IV. of 1843, Act VI. of 1845, Acts VIII. & IX. of 1849, and Act VII. of 1853.

¶ See Morley's Administration of Justice in India, p. 40.

Presidency, except that, as regards crimes and offences triable by jury, and committed by British officers or soldiers at places more than 120 miles from the seat of Government, they were not called upon to interfere, such crimes being cognizable by a Court Martial.

(3.) All persons who had committed crimes or offences at sea.

Lastly. All persons whatever resident without the jurisdiction of the Supreme Courts and the Court of the Recorder of Prince of Wales' Island were subject to the jurisdiction of Magistrates and Joint Magistrates acting as Justices of the Peace in certain cases. The law regulating the appointment and powers of Justices of the Peace was subsequently laid down by Act II. of 1869, and afterwards by the Code of Criminal Procedure.

Presidency Town Magistrates.

Magistrates of Police for the Presidency Towns were first appointed under Act XIII. of 1856. The Act required that they should be previously made Justices of the Peace; and gave to each of them all the powers and jurisdiction which are by law vested in two Justices of the Peace.

Both by the Code of Criminal Procedure passed in 1861 * and previously thereto, European British subjects could only be committed or held to bail for trial by a Justice of the Peace. A Magistrate (not being a Justice of the Peace) could only hear the complaint, issue a warrant of arrest, and hold him to bail with a view to the complaint being investigated by a Justice of the Peace.

The functions of a Justice of the Peace were threefold: first, the trial and punishment under certain Acts and Statutes † of offences by summary conviction, and without a jury; secondly, the investigation of charges in view to the committal or discharge of the accused person; and thirdly, the prevention of crime and breaches of the peace.

* Act XXV. of 1861, sec. 39.

† See 53 Geo. III. c. 155; Act VII. of 1853; and Criminal Procedure Code, 1861, sections 163 and 165.

LECTURE VI.

Coroners.

By the 157th section of the Statute noted below,* it was recited that it was expedient that Coroners should be appointed for the settlements in India for taking inquests upon view of the bodies of persons coming or supposed to have come to an untimely end. Power was accordingly given to the three Governments within their several Presidencies to appoint by order in Council certain British subjects to be Coroners, and by like orders to supersede or remove them as occasion might require. They were in respect of their powers and jurisdiction within the limits of the settlements for which they were appointed placed on a similar footing to Coroners elected for any county or place in England.

All the Judges of the Supreme Court were made Coroners as well as Justices of the Peace for their respective Presidencies.

The law relating to Coroners and their juries was laid down in certain subsequent † Acts; but that which at present regulates their proceedings and the jurisdiction of Coroners is laid down in a later Act of the Imperial Legislative Council, *viz.* Act IV. of 1871, amended as will be mentioned hereafter.

Rival judicial institutions.

Of the period of time which I have just had under consideration (1781—1861), half a century was marked by as wide a separation, as was compatible with social order, between the judicial authorities which controlled British-born subjects and ruled in the Presidency Towns and those which regulated the provinces and generally speaking the affairs of Natives. That separation originated in the peculiar circumstances under which a Company became as it were the rival of the Crown, and when once established, appealed to the prejudices of conquest and resisted all attempts to alter or abolish it. The Crown from the earliest introduction of its subjects into the country provided for the administration

* 33 Geo. III. c. 52.

† Acts XLV. of 1850, IV. of 1848, and XXVI. of 1848.

of justice amongst them by a system analogous to that which existed at home. The design of the Regulating Act was eventually to extend that system over the conquered country. It signally failed, and was from the first impossible. The Company, in the exercise of the sovereign power which it derived from the Mogul Emperor through the grant of the Dewanny, established a system of Courts suited to the wants of the country, but having no power over those who owed no allegiance to the Mogul. A compromise was made in 1781, by which the power of the Crown Courts was restricted, and the tribunals of the Company were recognized by Parliament. Thenceforward time and policy favoured amalgamation, but numerous circumstances and strong party feeling tended to prevent or delay it.

I shall in the next two lectures sketch the history of the Provincial Civil and Criminal Courts which were established by the Company. This, however, will be a convenient place to note the various encroachments which were made upon the exclusive jurisdiction over Europeans which belonged to the Courts established by Royal Charter, and the attempts which were made to transfer some portion of it to the rival institutions of the Company.

Tendency to amalgamation.

In 1813 the first step was taken to vest the Company's Courts with civil jurisdiction over British subjects and destroy that complete independence of the local Courts which Europeans had previously possessed. It was enacted * in that year by Parliament that British subjects residing, trading, or holding immovable property in the provinces should be amenable to the Civil Courts in suits brought against them by Natives. Even then their distinctive privilege of exemption was not entirely lost sight of, and the right was given to them of appeal to the Supreme Court in cases where Natives had the right of appeal to the Sudder Court.

* 53 Geo. III. c. 155, s. 107.

LECTURE VI.

In 1836* after the establishment of the Legislature of 1834, an Act was passed which repealed the provision just quoted of the Statute of George III. invidiously giving a right of appeal to the Supreme Court. It enacted that no person by reason of birth or descent should be exempt from the civil jurisdiction of certain of the Company's Courts therein specified, the number of which was increased by later legislation.†

No further step was taken towards a uniform administration of civil justice till the union of the Sudder and Supreme Courts was effected by Act of Parliament.

The general exemption of Europeans from the criminal jurisdiction of the provincial Courts remained till the Criminal Procedure Code of 1872. The earlier Code, and the Indian High Courts Act, both passed in 1861, recognized and preserved that exemption. And the powers of the old Supreme Court, derived from its Charter and from analogy to the Court of Queen's Bench, were retained by the High Court in its original jurisdiction.

Circumstances, however, led to that exemption being slowly and reluctantly challenged. By the Statute of George III., to which ‡ I have frequently referred, the Magistrates in the provinces were authorized to act as Justices of the Peace, and to have jurisdiction over British subjects out of the Presidency Town in certain criminal cases, and also in cases of small debts due by them to Natives. After the Legislature of 1834 was established, the jurisdiction of such Magistrates was gradually increased.§ The Mahomedan Code of Criminal

* Act XI. of 1836.

† See Acts XXIV. of 1836, III. of 1839, VI. of 1843, and III. of 1850.

‡ 53 Geo. III. c. 155.

§ See Acts XXXII. of 1838 and IX. of 1849, Act IV. of 1743, Act VII. of 1853.

Law was gradually disused, and since 1861 the Penal Code has applied alike to Europeans and Natives. Lecture VI.

Conclusion.

At the present day, that is, since 1872, Englishmen and Natives are subject in civil matters to the same Courts and to the same procedure; in criminal matters, to the same substantive law, and the same appellate authority, but in a great degree to different Courts for purposes of commitment and trial. The Criminal Procedure Code of 1872 re-cast the Criminal Courts, and effected a considerable advance towards uniformity of criminal administration, preserving, however, to European British subjects such privileges as policy and safety seemed to require.

LECTURE VII.

LATER HISTORY: THE PROVINCIAL CIVIL COURTS.

Foundation of Civil Courts—Establishment of Supreme Court—Rival establishments of the Company—Changes in the scheme of 1772—Native authority restored—Effect of the changes—Separation in 1780 of Civil and Revenue Jurisdiction—Struggles between Civil and Revenue Courts—Sudder Dewanny Adawlut—Finally established by Act of Parliament—Re-union in 1787 of Civil and Revenue Jurisdiction by Lord Cornwallis—Changes in the Courts to effect that object—Second separation in 1793 of Civil and Revenue Jurisdiction—Reasons for that separation—Duties of Collectors—Reorganization of Civil Courts—Sudder Dewanny Adawlut—Provincial Courts of Appeal—Courts of Dewanny Adawlut—Lower grades of Judges—Changes in the Civil Courts in 1831—Gradual re-union 1793—1831 of Civil and Revenue Jurisdiction—First step towards re-union—Second step—Third step—Civil and Revenue Jurisdiction united for the third time (1831)—Further extension of the Collector's jurisdiction—Suits cognizable by the Collectors under Act X. of 1859—Control over the Collectors—Opposition to the passing of Act X. of 1859—Consequences of the Act—Third separation of Civil and Revenue Jurisdiction—Act VIII. of 1869 (B. C.)—Further History of the Civil Courts—Madras Courts—Inferior tribunals—Bombay Courts—Revenue jurisdiction in both Presidencies.

Foundation of Civil Courts.

THE earliest proceeding of any importance, with reference to the establishment of provincial Courts for the administration of civil justice, was the report of Warren Hastings and the scheme which was prepared in 1772.* A leading feature, it will be remembered, of that scheme was the union of fiscal and judicial authority in the same officers.

Then followed the policy already described which led to

* See *ante*, page 28.

the establishment of the Supreme Court, and the disastrous results of the first few years of its administration. The plan, if ever it had been formed, as there seems reason to suspect, of drawing into the hands of the new Court the superintendence of the whole administration of justice, had obviously failed. So also had failed Mr. Sullivan's scheme for establishing a somewhat similar Court, whose members were to be appointed by the Company, and which it was intended should bring the whole of the Native Courts into subordination to it.* A Court therefore was established, whose jurisdiction extended over all the vast territories included in the Presidency of Fort William, but which was isolated from the general Courts of the country, over which it failed to acquire any influence or authority. It had a personal jurisdiction thinly scattered over a dense population and a wide extent of country. It enforced that jurisdiction, issued its writs, seized and sold lands and property in the midst of people who lived under a different law and procedure from those observed by the Court, and were subordinate to other tribunals.

Establishment of Supreme Court.

Contemporaneously with the establishment of the Presidency Town system which I have described in the last lecture, and which emanated mostly from the Crown and Parliament, the Company had striven to establish a system for the administration of justice throughout the Mofussil. I shall now proceed to sketch the history of the civil and criminal institutions which were so established, and by aid of which, with occasional interference from the powers which belonged to the rival system, the Company endeavoured to rule the three Presidencies which they had acquired.

Rival establishments of the Company

The Regulating Act led to numerous alterations in the scheme of Warren Hastings; for the Governor-General was out-voted by a majority of his Council who had recently

Changes in the scheme of 1772.

* Fifth Appendix to Third Report of Select Committee, 1831; Sir C. Grey's Minute, pp. 1142, 1145.

LECTURE VII. arrived from England. The changes which they made in the Civil Courts were as follows:—In 1775 the superintendence of the collection of the revenue was vested in six provincial Councils, appointed for the respective divisions of Calcutta, Burdwan, Dacca, Moorshedabad, Dinagepore, and Patna; and the administration of civil justice was transferred from the European Collectors, who were recalled, to Native Amils who were appointed instead. From them an appeal lay in every case to the new provincial Councils, and thence under certain restrictions to the Governor-General and Council as the Sudder Adawlut.

Native authority restored. In the same year the Directors urged and effected the restoration of Mahomed Reza Khan to the high office which he had held at Moorshedabad, and from which he had been dismissed by Mr. Hastings.*

The majority of the Council were in favour of again making him in name and title the Naib Subah, *i.e.* in effect recognizing the existence of the Nabob's government, deeming that step politic for managing discussions with foreign factories. Mr. Hastings unsuccessfully opposed it, saying "that the Nabob is a mere pageant, without the shadow of authority, and even his most consequential agents receive their express nomination from the servants of the Company." The Judges of the Supreme Court had held the same thing, when a servant of the Nabob's claimed exemption from their jurisdiction as an ambassador. "I do not," said Mr. Hastings, "remember any instance and I hope none will be found, of our having been so disingenuous as to disclaim our own power, or to affirm that the Nabob is the real sovereign of those provinces."

Mahomed Reza Khan † was removed again in 1778, after Mr. Hastings had, through the death of one of his colleagues,

* Mill's History of England, Vol. III., p. 455.

† Mill's History of India, Vol. IV., p. 20.

become, with the aid of his own casting-vote, supreme in the Government.

LECTURE VII.

Effect of the changes.

The effect of the alterations made in 1775, taken together with the transference of the Nizamut Adawlut from Calcutta to Moorshedabad, was to revive to some extent the Native Government for the purpose of administering civil and criminal justice, probably with a view to elude the interference of the Supreme Court, and to effect a considerable separation between that department and the business of revenue collection and management.

Separation in 1780 of civil and revenue jurisdiction.

In 1780 regulations were passed in pursuance of the legislative authority granted by the Regulating Act, and by those regulations the separation just referred to between the judicial and revenue authority was completed. The jurisdiction of the six provincial Councils was confined exclusively to revenue matters;* and it was resolved that, for the more effectual and regular administration of civil justice, district Courts of Dewanny Adawlut should be established within the jurisdictions of the six provincial Councils. These Courts were to be independent of the Councils, and to exercise jurisdiction over all claims of inheritance to zemindaries, talookdaries, and other real property, or mercantile disputes, and all matters of personal property; all cases regarding revenue or rent being reserved for the exclusive cognizance of the provincial Councils or of the Collectors† who superseded them.

Eighteen of these Dewanny Adawluts were established. Regulations for their guidance were drawn up by Sir Elijah Impey, and incorporated in a revised Code. The ultimate appeal lay to the Sudder Dewanny Adawlut. And shortly after this distinct separation of civil justice from revenue

* Reg. I., 1780, s. 3.

† See Harrington's Analysis, Vol. I., p. 31.

LECTURE VII.

collection, the Supreme Court was deprived of the right to interfere in matters concerning the revenue.

Thus, in seven years from the date of Warren Hastings' scheme, which united in the same hands fiscal and judicial powers, a considerable alteration was made in the constitution of the tribunals of civil justice. The period had been conspicuous for the conflict which had been carried on between the Supreme Court and the Governor-General's Council, which resulted in the Act of Parliament of 1781. Experience seemed to suggest that it was advisable to divide the business of the provincial tribunals into two parts; that which peculiarly concerned the revenue, and that which peculiarly concerned individuals. The former continued to be preserved to the provincial Councils, that is to the Collectors who eventually superseded them: but they were exonerated from the burden of adjudicating upon private disputes, which was transferred to separate Courts styled the Dewanny Adawluts.

Struggles between Civil and Revenue Courts.

Then there ensued a struggle between the Civil and Revenue Courts, insignificant, no doubt, as compared with the civil war which raged between the Supreme Court and the Supreme Council, but sufficient to engage the serious attention of Government. The rival claims of the Revenue and Civil Courts to exercise jurisdiction, were destined to a long antagonism and to varying success. It is interesting to to observe that, within a few months of the separation of their functions, the Governor-General penned a minute,* which said:—"The institution of the new Courts of Dewanny Adawlut has already given occasion to very troublesome and alarming competition between them and the provincial Councils." The history of the Civil Courts of this country involves a narrative of these struggles which ensued between the revenue authorities and the judicial officers to gain exclusive jurisdiction.

* Mill's History of India, Vol. IV., p. 245.

Sudder Dewanny Adawlut.

From the first, however, the business of the Sudder Dewanny Adawlut was described to be not only to receive appeals from these Courts, but to superintend their conduct, revise their proceedings, remedy their defects, and generally to form such new regulations and checks as experience should prove to be necessary to the purpose of their institution. In 1780 the Chief Justice of the Supreme Court was appointed Judge of the Sudder Dewanny Adawlut, and was vested with all its powers. The Governor-General and Council, who previously formed that Adawlut, ceased to belong to it, but it was expressly stipulated that the Chief Justice should enjoy the office and salary at their pleasure. The Chief Justice, in fulfilment of the duties which devolved upon him by virtue of his new office, prepared a series of regulations for the guidance of the Civil Courts, which were afterwards incorporated in a revised Code passed in 1781.

Finally established by Act of Parliament.

In the same year, that is in 1781, the Sudder Dewanny Adawlut was constituted by Act of Parliament * a Court of Record. Although it was not established by Royal Charter, it was nevertheless distinguished from the ordinary Courts of the Company, and traced its final establishment to the recognition and sanction of the Imperial Parliament. In the next year the Court of Directors sent out orders to the Governor-General in Council to resume the superintendence of that Court.

Re-union in 1787 of civil and revenue jurisdiction by Lord Cornwallis.

Lord Cornwallis came to India as Governor-General in 1786. Previous to his arrival, an Act of Parliament † had established a Board of Commissioners for the Affairs of India, and had directed enquiries to be made as to the grievances of the Natives. Lord Cornwallis brought with him instructions from the Court of Directors, dictated with a view to carry out the object of Parliament, which was, in the words of the

* 21 Geo. III. c. 70, s. 71.

† 24 Geo. III. c. 25.

LECTURE VII.

Act, "to establish permanent rules for the settlement and collection of the revenue, and for the administration of justice founded on the ancient laws and local usages of the country."

He accordingly directed the re-union of the functions of civil and criminal justice with those of the collection and management of the revenue. He placed the Dewanny Adawluts under the superintendence of the Collectors; he resolved in Council to resume the superintendence of the administration of criminal justice throughout the provinces; and after a few years removed to Calcutta the Nizamut Adawlut which had been, during the time of Warren Hastings, transferred to Moorshedabad. Although the functions of civil justice and of the collection of the revenue were re-united in the person of the Collectors, the Courts over which they presided were kept distinct. Lord Cornwallis's policy, apparently, was to revive the institutions which had been framed in pursuance of the scheme of 1772 and to carry out the intentions of Warren Hastings before the changes made by the Council led to the adoption of a different system.

Changes in the Courts to effect that object.

It was in * the year 1787 that it was resolved, in obedience to the Court of Directors, that the office of Judge of the several Mofussil Courts (except those which were established in the cities of Patna, Moorshedabad, and Dacca) should be held by the person who had charge of the Revenue; and in the same year a revised code of judicial regulations adapted to this change of system was published. All revenue cases were by this code assigned to the Collector, from whom an appeal lay to the Board of Revenue, and ultimately to the Governor-General in Council. The object of thus reverting to the system which had been discontinued in 1780 was to accustom the Natives to look to one master. It was considered impossible, after the experience of seven years, to

* Harrington's Analysis, Vol. I., p. 32.

draw a line between the revenue and judicial departments in such a manner as to prevent their clashing. The then existing regulations had endeavoured to do so, but constant confusion was the result.

Second separation in 1793 of civil and revenue jurisdiction.

But then came a third change of policy.* In a minute of Lord Cornwallis, published in 1793, he said:—"There is no class of men which Government should watch with greater jealousy, and on whom the regulations should have a stricter control, than the officers who are entrusted with the collection of the public revenue. It is necessary to arm them with power to enforce their demands, * * *; but to prevent the abuse of this power, there should be Courts of Justice ready to punish oppression and exaction." The experience of six years induced Lord Cornwallis to return to the system of separation of the fiscal and judicial systems which he found in existence on his arrival.

Accordingly in the same year he established a complete system of judicature throughout the Presidency of Bengal, and formed the existing regulations into a regular code. The chief feature of the new system was the abolition of the Revenue Courts and the transference of all causes hitherto tried by the revenue officers to the Civil Courts; thus entirely separating the collection of revenue from the administration of justice, which were thenceforth confided to separate offices.

Reasons for that separation.

"All questions," said the preamble to the regulation † which carried out this policy, "between Government and the landholders respecting the assessment and collection of the public revenue and disputed claims between the latter and their ryots, or other persons concerned in the collection of their rents, have hitherto been cognizable in the Courts of Maal Adawlut, or Revenue Courts. The Collectors of the Revenue preside in these Courts as Judges, and an appeal lies from

* Harrington's Analysis, Vol. I., p. 42.

† Reg. II. of 1793.

LECTURE VII.

their decision to the Board of Revenue, and from the decrees of that Board to the Governor-General in Council in the department of revenue.

"The proprietors can never consider the privileges which have been conferred upon them as secure whilst the revenue officers are vested with these judicial powers. Exclusive of the objections arising to these Courts from their irregular, summary and often *ex parte* proceedings, and from the Collectors being obliged to suspend the exercise of their judicial functions whenever they interfere with their financial duties; it is obvious that, if the regulations for assessing and collecting the public revenue are infringed, the revenue officers themselves must be the aggressors, and that individuals who have been wronged by them in one capacity can never hope to obtain redress from them in another. Their financial occupations equally disqualify them for administering the laws between the proprietors of land and their tenants.

"Other security, therefore, must be given to landed property and to the rights attached to it, before the desired improvements in agriculture can be expected to be effected. Government must divest itself of the power of infringing in its executive capacity the rights and privileges which, as exercising the legislative authority, it has conferred on the landholders. The revenue officers must be deprived of their judicial powers. All financial claims of the public, when disputed under the regulations, must be subjected to the cognizance of Courts of Judicature, superintended by Judges who, from their official situations and the nature of their trusts, shall not only be wholly uninterested in the result of their decisions, but bound to decide impartially between the public and the proprietors of land, and also between the latter and their tenants. The Collectors of the Revenue must not only be divested of the power of deciding upon their own acts, but rendered amenable for them to the Courts of Judicature, and must collect the public dues subject to a personal prosecution for every exaction exceeding the amount which they are authorized to demand on behalf of the public and for every deviation from the regulations prescribed for the collection of it."

It must be admitted that this preamble lays down a sound and reasonable policy, founded upon strict justice, necessary for the due preservation and security of what are called landed interests. But although that policy was immediately carried out by Lord Cornwallis, constant attempts were successfully made in the interests of the Executive to depart from it in later times. In 1831 we shall find that those jurisdictions were again united, and that later on Act X. of 1859 was passed, which directly violates the principles and policy laid down in the preamble to that famous regulation.

Duties of Collectors.

The Collectors were thenceforth entrusted with the collection of the revenue payable to Government as executive officers subordinate to the Board of Revenue. The nature of their duties was described in Section 8, Regulation II. of 1793.

Re-organization of Civil Courts.

Having thus confined the Collectors to their exclusively executive functions, the next step was to re-organize the Civil Courts of Justice and render them efficient and independent. Accordingly, by the next regulation,* Government, in the language of its preamble, divested itself "of the power of interfering in the administration of the laws and regulations in the first instance, reserving only as a Court of Appeal or Review the decision of certain cases in the last resort;" and lodged its judicial authority in Courts of Justice.

Sudder Dewanny Adawlut.

By Regulation VI. of 1793, the Sudder Dewanny Adawlut was re-established at the Presidency, and consisted of the Governor-General and the other members of the Supreme Council. It received appeals from the provincial Courts and

* Reg. III. of 1793.

LECTURE VII.

Councils and from the Board of Revenue. In 1801, it was made to consist of three Judges, appointed by the Governor-General, the chief being also a member of the Supreme Council, the other two being selected from the covenanted servants of the Company; * and in 1811 (see Regulation XII.) of a Chief Judge and as many Puisne Judges as the Governor-General in Council should think necessary. The powers and duties of the Court were defined by the Regulations of 1793 and 1801; and were extended by later legislation over Benares and the Ceded Provinces.†

In 1831 a Sudder ‡ Dewanny Adawlut was constituted for the North-Western Provinces with similar powers.

Provincial Courts of Appeal.

Four provincial Courts of Appeal were established (Regulation V. of 1793) within the provinces of Bengal, Behar, and Orissa for the purpose of hearing appeals from the several zillah and city Courts next mentioned; the Sudder Dewanny Adawlut being vested with appellate jurisdiction and general power of supervision over the inferior Courts in all suits above Rs. 1000. By later regulations two more provincial Courts were established; one for the province of Benares, and one for the Ceded Provinces.

Courts of Dewanny Adawlut.

Courts of Dewanny Adawlut for the trial of civil suits in the first instance were by Regulation III. of 1793 established in twenty-three zillahs and three cities. It defined their jurisdiction, and directed the Judges of those Courts to act when no specific rule existed according to justice, equity, and good conscience; while Regulation IV. prescribed their procedure. In 1795 and 1803 similar Courts were established in the Benares and Ceded Provinces. These regulations were all repealed by Act X. of 1861. The Provincial Courts

* Reg. II. of 1801.

† See Reg. X. of 1795 and V. of 1803.

‡ Reg. VI. of 1831.

themselves were abolished in pursuance of Regulation II. of 1833.

Lower grades of Judges.

Below the city and zillah Courts were two classes of inferior Judges. First in order, the Registers of those Courts who could decide causes for amounts not exceeding Rs. 200, subject to revision by the Judge. The next and lowest grade of Judges were the Native Commissioners, who under Regulation XL. of 1793 could decide civil suits for sums of money or personal property of a value not exceeding 50 Sicca rupees. Of these officers, the head Commissioners were called Sudder Ameens, and the rest were called Moonsiffs.

This was the general outline of the new system which was established for the administration of civil justice. The year 1793 marks the era of independence in that administration. The Government endeavoured to separate between their judicial and executive functions and to render the officers who performed the latter functions amenable to the authority of those who exercised the former duties. The Courts so established lasted most of them for a considerable space of time, nearly eighty years, but by the process of occasional extension and repeal the statutory provisions which created them were enveloped in some obscurity.

Changes in the Civil Courts in 1831.

Some alterations in detail were made during subsequent years. Regulation XXIII. of 1814 consolidated the several rules which had been passed regarding the office of the Native Commissioners; modified and extended their powers in the trial and decision of civil suits; authorized the Judges of the zillah and city Courts to employ them in the execution of certain additional duties; and transferred to the provincial Courts the control over their appointment and removal which had been formerly exercised by the Sudder Dewanny Adawlut.

At length, in 1831, Regulation V. of that year made some important alterations. The object was recited in the

LECTURE VII.

preamble to be the gradual introduction of respectable Natives into the more important trusts connected with the administration of the country. Moonsiffs were invested with power to try and determine suits for money and other personal property of the value of Rs. 300, suits with regard to land of the value of Rs. 300, except such land as was exempt from the payment of revenue. The Judges were empowered to refer to the Sudder Ameens any suits which did not exceed Rs. 1000. Principal Sudder Ameens were also authorized to be appointed, to whom suits might be referred not exceeding Rs. 5000. Registers' Courts were abolished; provincial Courts of Appeal were gradually superseded, and in two years finally abolished; and original jurisdiction was given to the Judges in all suits exceeding in value Rs. 5000, with an appeal direct to the Sudder Dewanny Adawlut. All the procedure provisions contained in these and preceding regulations were repealed, and one general code upon that subject was first established by Act VIII. of 1859.

Gradual re-union 1793—1831 of civil and revenue jurisdiction.

During this time, that is in the period which intervened between 1793 and 1831, the relations of the Collectors to the Civil Courts underwent considerable alterations.

The system of 1793, which, to all appearance, had finally severed the work of administering justice from that of collecting revenue, had provided,* in order to ensure expedition, that the Judges of the zillah and city Courts might refer petty suits to their Registers, or as they came to be called in later times Sudder Ameens, or Principal Sudder Ameens, as the case might be. Advantage was taken of this circumstance in the very next year to re-invest the revenue officers with some of the power which they had lost. It was the duty of the Judges to revise the orders of the Registers, and to countersign them before they were considered to be valid. The work of revision was found to be as long as that of trying

First step towards re-union.

* See Reg. XIII. of 1793.

in the first instance. And so it was enacted by Regulation VIII. of 1794 that the Courts might refer to the Collectors all cases which, before the new system, had been cognizable by them. The Collectors were thereupon bound to send in their report, which the Judge might confirm or set aside, or he might make any order thereon that he might think fit. This was the commencement of a re-transfer to the Collectors of judicial functions; increased authority being required, as it was urged, to enable them to obtain payment of the Government revenue.

Second step.

In the next year, a summary procedure was provided for the determination of claims to arrears of rent. This was superseded by Regulation VII. of 1799, which for a long time formed the basis of summary suit law. It was recited in that regulation that the powers of the landholders for enforcing payment of rents had been in some cases found insufficient, and that considerable delay had occurred in payment of Government revenue. It referred to the summary process of recovery given by Regulation XXXV. of 1793, and enacted several rules in lieu thereof. It enforced the strictest observance of the rule laid down in Regulation VII. of 1793, that the Civil Courts were to give priority to rent and revenue cases. They were still authorized to refer cases for report to the Collectors, and afterwards to adjudicate upon them. The object of the regulation was to enable landed proprietors to realize their rents speedily, with a view to punctual payment of Government revenue.

Again, in 1812,* a summary remedy was given to the ryot against his landlord in all cases in which he was aggrieved by distress for rent. The cognizance of such cases was also practically vested in the Collector, to whom they were ordered to be referred.

* See Reg. V. of 1812.

LECTURE VII.

Third step.

And in 1824, about thirty years after Lord Cornwallis' policy had been carried into effect, an important regulation * was passed, which recited that the provisions contained in the regulations then in force empowering the Judges of the zillah and city Courts to refer accounts and summary suits to the Collectors for report, had been found insufficient to expedite trials. It was considered by the Legislature to be indispensable to the attainment of that object that the revenue officers should be vested with authority to hear, investigate, and determine by a summary process, and subject to a regular suit in the Civil Court, all rent suits which might be referred to them by the Judges. Rules were enacted in this regulation for their guidance, and the same powers were given to them as were vested in the Civil Courts, for compelling the attendance and the examination of witnesses, and generally for all process, except execution of their decrees, which was confided to the Civil Courts.

Civil and revenue jurisdiction united for the third time (1831).

This was followed in 1831 by another regulation, which deprived the Judges of all jurisdiction over summary suits relating to rent, and transferred them to the exclusive cognizance of the Collectors, whose decisions were to be final, subject to a regular suit, which was to be brought in the Civil Court. The Commissioner could revise the decision of the Collectors, solely on the ground of the case not being of a nature cognizable as a summary suit.

Thus in 1831 rent and revenue cases were again transferred to the Collectors, in order to facilitate the collection of Government revenue. No rules, however, for conducting the summary inquiry, either before the Civil Courts or before the Collectors, had ever been laid down. Considerable oppression resulted from this state of things, the tenants not being sufficiently protected from the landlord, and the landlord not being sufficiently protected from the Collectors.

* Reg. XIV. of 1824.

Further extension of the Collector's jurisdiction.

In 1857 a Bill was introduced into the Legislative Council of India, with a view to enlarge and define the jurisdiction of the Collectors, with respect to summary suits for arrears or exactions of rent, and generally with respect to the law regulating the relations of landlord and tenant. The Collector was considered to be the person most deeply interested in promoting this branch of the administration of civil justice, being best acquainted with the fiscal state of the district, with the tenures prevailing in it, and with the character of the landlords. The Bill gave to the revenue officers exclusively the primary cognizance of all cases of ejectment, cancelment of leases for arrears of rent, enhancement of rent, and right of demanding pottahs and kubooleuts.

As the law stood before that Bill, the Civil Courts, and not the revenue officers, had jurisdiction to try suits for the delivery of pottahs or kubooleuts, or for the determination of the rates of rent at which such pottahs or kubooleuts ought to be delivered, and also over all suits in ejectment, or to cancel a lease for non-payment of rent, or for breach of conditions of any contract involving a liability to ejectment or cancelment of a lease. Collectors and Deputy Collectors, therefore, it was proposed should acquire a still greater portion of the jurisdiction of the Civil Courts than they had previously obtained under the Regulations of 1824 and 1831.

Suits cognizable by the Collectors under Act X. of 1859.

The Bill became law in 1859, being Act X. in that year passed by the Governor-General in Council. It provided in the 23rd Section that the following suits should be cognizable by the Collectors of Land Revenue, and should be instituted and tried under the provisions of that Act, and except in the way of appeal as therein provided, should not be cognizable in any other Court, or by any other officer, or in any other manner:—*

(1.) All suits for the delivery of pottahs or kubooleuts, or

* Section 23.

Lecture VII.

for the determination of the rates of rent at which such pottahs or kubooleuts are to be delivered.

(2.) All suits for damages on account of the illegal exaction of rent, or of any unauthorized cess or impost, or on account of the refusal of receipts for rent paid, or on account of the extortion of rent by confinement or other duress.

(3.) All complaints of excess in demand of rent, and all claims to abatement of rent.

(4.) All suits for arrears of rent due on account of land either kherajee or lakheraj, or on account of any rights of pasturage, forest rights, fisheries, or the like.

(5.) All suits to eject any ryot, or to cancel any lease on account of the non-payment of arrears of rent, or on account of a breach of the conditions of any contract by which a ryot may be liable to ejectment, or a lease may be liable to be cancelled.

(6.) All suits to recover the occupancy or possession of any land, farm or tenure, from which a ryot, farmer or tenant has been illegally ejected by the person entitled to receive rent for the same.

(7.) All suits arising out of the exercise of the power of distraint conferred on zemindars and others by the Act,* or out of any acts done under colour of the exercise of the said power as hereinafter particularly provided.

(8.) All suits by zemindars and others in receipt of the rent of land against any agents employed by them in the management of land, or collection of rents, or the sureties of such agents for money received, or accounts kept by such agents in the course of such employment, or for papers in their possession.

Control over the Collectors.

In the performance of their duties under the Act, the Collectors and Deputy Collectors, so far as these latter are vested with any powers thereunder, are rendered subject to

* See Sections 112 and 114.

the general direction and control of the Commissioners and the Boards of Revenue. And the Deputy Collectors are placed under the direction and control of the Collectors to whom they are subordinate. Appeals are allowed in certain cases from the Deputy Collector to the Collector, and from the Collector to the Commissioner. Orders passed in appeal by a Commissioner or a Collector are not open to any further appeal, but the Board of Revenue or the Commissioner may call for any case, and pass such orders thereupon as they may think fit. A Collector's decree is not appealable if for money below Rs. 100, unless the decision involves some question of right to enhance rents or some question relating to a title to land.

Opposition to the passing of Act X. of 1859. Mr. Peacock strongly opposed the passing of the 23rd Section, which took away the jurisdiction of the Civil Court, and transferred so many suits to the exclusive cognizance of the revenue officers. He objected to abolishing the jurisdiction of the Civil Courts, and also to the competency of the revenue officers to exercise this new jurisdiction, and he pointed out that the object of Regulation VIII. of 1831 appeared to be to encourage regular suits in a Civil Court, rather than summary suits before a Collector when the law gave an option. Mr. Peacock and Sir Charles Jackson recorded their dissent from the Bill, on the ground that it invested the revenue authorities with power to try the suits between landlord and tenant, and deprived the regular Civil Courts of their jurisdiction, notwithstanding that the suits might involve difficult questions of law and fact.

Consequences of the Act. The consequence of Act X. of 1859 was found to be that cases involving difficult and intricate points of law, and concerning important interests in land, came on for adjudication before Collectors and their subordinates, and it soon appeared that such officers were thereby entrusted with work of more

LECTURE VII.

difficulty and responsibility than was suited to their official knowledge and experience.

Third separation of civil and revenue jurisdiction.

In ten years from the date of that Act, notwithstanding the familiarity with that class of cases which time had brought to the Collectors and their deputies, the Bengal Legislative Council passed an Act (VIII. of 1869) which authorized the transfer of the jurisdiction to hear and determine them back again to the Civil Courts; which Courts were to accept the procedure of the Civil Procedure Code with a few modifications, such as the nature of the subject required. All suits which, under Act X. of 1859, were triable by Collectors of Land Revenue, were under the later Act transferred to the cognizance of the Civil Courts. The Act took effect in those districts in the Lower Provinces of Bengal to which it is extended by order of the Governor-General published in the *Calcutta Gazette*. In districts so mentioned the jurisdiction of the Collectors to entertain civil suits, under Act X. of 1859 and Bengal Act VI. of 1862, ceased save as regards any suits or proceedings then pending before them; and it was enacted that all suits brought for any cause of action arising under either of those Acts, or under Act VIII. of 1869, should be cognizable by the Civil Courts in those places according to their several jurisdictions. In 1885 the Bengal Tenancy Act was passed by the Governor-General of India in Council and repealed the whole of Act X. of 1859 and Act VIII. of 1869. Under the 13th Chapter of this Act the Civil Courts have jurisdiction in all matters between landlord and tenant; and the procedure and appeals in all rent suits are regulated thereby.

Act XVIII. of 1873.

Act XVIII. of 1873, however, which was passed for the North-West Provinces, though it repeals Act X. of 1859, consolidated and amended that and its amending Acts, and preserved to the Revenue Courts exclusive jurisdiction. Subsequently Act XII. of 1881 pursued the same course.

Settlement Officers continue to be, from time to time, in different parts of India, vested with civil jurisdiction in rent cases to the exclusion of the Civil Courts.

Further history of the Civil Courts.

Having thus traced the progress of rivalry between the Civil and Revenue Courts, it only remains to state that the Adawlut system was revised and placed upon a definite footing by the Bengal Civil Courts Act of 1871, which I shall hereafter describe when I come to treat of the existing judicial system. The course of legislation was found to have introduced considerable confusion as to the functions of the Judges and the constitution and jurisdiction of the Courts. In order to ascertain them it had become necessary to trace out and piece together various bits of legislation which were distributed over no less than thirteen different enactments. Mr. Fitzjames Stephen * thus in 1871 described the statutory basis of the existing Courts. First of all there were two regulations in 1793, large parts of which had been repealed and amended and re-amended; what remained of each defined the jurisdiction and procedure of the zillah Courts of Lower Bengal, Patna, Dacca, and Moorshedabad. Then with regard to the regulations of the later years, the unrepealed bits of them when discovered applied a similar system to other cities and to the provinces ceded by the Nawab Nazim of Bengal to the East India Company, and finally other enactments purported to extend the same system to the conquered provinces situated within the Doab and on the right bank of the Jumna, and of the territory ceded by the Peishwa. A prolonged course of reading and of the examination and collation of different enactments was necessary before any man could discover what were the Courts that really existed in Bengal. The Legislature recognised the necessity of re-establishing them, and accordingly passed the Act of 1871.

* Legislative Proceedings of the Governor-General's Council, 1871, p. 87.

LECTURE VII.

Madras Courts.

In the Madras Presidency it appears that the Adawlut system, framed upon the plan of Lord Cornwallis adopted in Bengal, was introduced in the year 1802. The Civil and Revenue Courts were kept distinct. The Registers had jurisdiction to try suits referred to them by the Judge. The Judges could decide finally in suits under 1000 rupees in value. There were four provincial Courts of Appeal; and the Sudder Court consisted of the Governor in Council, with an appeal from him in suits of the value of 45,000 rupees to the Governor-General in Council. In 1806 the constitution of the Sudder Court was altered, and new Judges appointed.* And in 1807 the Governor was declared to be no longer a Judge.†

Inferior tribunals.

In 1816 ‡ a regulation was passed by the local Legislature, in pursuance of which heads of villages were appointed Moonsiffs, with power to try and finally determine suits not exceeding Rs. 10 in value. They were also authorized to assemble village punchayets for the adjudication of civil suits of any amount within their village jurisdictions; the majority to decide. Another regulation § empowered the provincial Courts to annul the decision of the punchayets, and to refer to a second punchayet, whose decision, if it agreed with the former one, was to be final.

In 1843 the provincial Courts of Appeal were abolished.‖ New zillah Courts were established and the jurisdiction of the subordinate Judges and principal Sudder Ameens was increased so as to include all suits of less value than 10,000 rupees. Such Courts were to have jurisdiction over Europeans and Americans as well as Natives, and

* Regulation IV. of 1806.
† Regulation III. of 1807.
‡ Regulation IV. of 1816.
§ Regulation V. of 1807.
‖ Act VII. of 1843.

an appeal lay from them to the zillah Judges. Eventually Act III. of 1873 established, as is hereafter stated, a system of Courts similar to those planted in Bengal by Act VI. of 1871.

Bombay Courts.

With regard to the Adawlut system in the Bombay Presidency, it appears that the Court of Directors in 1794 transmitted to the Government of that Presidency a copy of the regulations proposed by Lord Cornwallis for the internal government of the Bengal provinces; and eventually, Courts of Civil and Criminal Judicature were constituted by the Bombay Government on principles similar to those on which the Courts in the Presidency of Bengal had been established. In 1827 all the Bombay regulations passed previously to that year, with few exceptions, were rescinded, and a new code was established by which the system of judicature was entirely remodelled, based however upon the Bengal Regulations of 1793. In 1845 the appointment of Joint zillah Judges, whenever the state of civil business required it, was authorized.*

The Civil Courts of Bombay, as they continued to exist for a considerable space of time, were constituted by regulations passed in the first seven years after the Revised Code of 1827, which enacted such modifications of the original system as experience suggested. Those regulations in turn were subjected to a constant process of partial repeal till the law and constitution of the Courts in Bombay as in Bengal were placed in a most unsatisfactory state. Act XIV. of 1869 was eventually passed, and constituted the Civil Courts of Bombay in a manner which I shall hereafter explain.

Revenue jurisdiction in both Presidencies.

It appears that both in Madras and Bombay the revenue officers had the power of trying all rent suits. From their decisions the appeal lay in the former Presidency to the zillah Courts; in the latter to the Sudder Court. In 1866

* Act XXIX. of 1845.

LECTURE VII.

the local Legislature at Bombay passed an Act * to divest the Courts of Revenue of jurisdiction in cases relating to the rent of land and the use of wells, tanks, watercourses, and roads to fields, and to vest such jurisdiction in the Civil Courts.

* Act II. of 1866 (Bombay C.).

LECTURE VIII.

LATER HISTORY—THE PROVINCIAL CRIMINAL COURTS.

Criminal Justice in early times—Sudder Nizamut Adawlut—Mahomedan law—Governor-General supersedes the Nawab Nazim—Police administration in early times—Scheme of Warren Hastings—Civil Judges appointed Magistrates—Further Measures—System of 1793—Sudder Nizamut Adawlut—Courts of Circuit—Abolished in 1829—Replaced by Commissioners of Revenue and Circuit—Criminal jurisdiction of Zillah Judges—Sessions Judges—Bengal Sessions Court Act of 1871—Act of 1872—Criminal Justice in Madras—Criminal Justice in Bombay—Sudder Nizamut for the North-West Provinces—Police in Bengal—Supervision of Police by Magistrates—Zillah Judges declared to be Magistrates—Police in Benares—Assimilated to Bengal—Police Officers—Darogahs—Mohurrahs—Jemadars—Watchers—Control by Commissioners of Circuit—Police in Madras—Police in Bombay—General condition of the Police—Sir Charles Napier's reform of it in Sind—North-West Provinces—Bombay and Punjab—Oudh—Madras—Act V. of 1861.

Criminal Justice in early times.

THE scheme for the administration of criminal as well as of civil justice in Bengal is attributable to Warren Hastings. The principle originally adopted was to retain the Mahomedan law and law officers and Courts for the repression of crime; subject to the supervision, not apparently very close or effective, of the Government. A scheme of police was also prepared and carried into execution. But in the year 1793 the whole system of criminal and police, as well as of civil, administration was remodelled, by the light of the experience of twenty years.

It appears * that Criminal Courts, denominated Foujdary Adawluts, were first appointed in Bengal for the trial of

* See Regulation IX. of 1793, Preamble.

persons charged with crimes or misdemeanours pursuant to the regulations passed by the President in Council in 1772. The Collectors of Revenue were directed to superintend the proceedings of the officers in those Courts, and on trials to see that the necessary witnesses were summoned and examined, that due weight was allowed to their testimony, and that the decisions passed were fair and impartial.

Sudder Nizamut Adawlut.

A Sudder Nizamut Adawlut was established at Moorshedabad under the superintendence of a Committee of Revenue for the purpose of revising the proceedings of the provincial Courts in capital cases. It was upon the abolition of that Committee that the Nizamut Adawlut was, for the first time, brought to Calcutta. The history of the provincial Criminal Courts down to the year 1775, when the Nizamut Adawlut was carried back to Moorshedabad, has already been described.* The Foujdary Adawluts, however, did not work successfully under the superintendence of the East India Company's Government; and the discharge of the duties entrusted to the Governor-General, as head of the Nizamut Adawlut or Supreme Penal Court of Calcutta, loaded him with a weight of business and of responsibility from † which he sought to be relieved. The majority of the Council took advantage of the circumstance to restore to Mahomed Reza Khan, the Mohamedan Dewan to whom I have frequently referred, the superintendence of penal justice and of the Criminal Courts throughout the country; and for that purpose, removed the seat of the Nizamut Adawlut from Calcutta back to Moorshedabad.

Mahomedan law.

During the fifteen years which elapsed before the Nizamut was again restored to Calcutta, the course of the administration of criminal justice, setting aside the jurisdiction of the Supreme Court, was that the Mahomedan tribunals

* See *ante*, pp. 27 and 29.

† Mill's History of India, Vol. III., p. 455.

administered Mahomedan law under the general control of the Nazim, but subject in each Court to the supervision of English authority.

Governor-General supersedes the Nawab Nazim.

In 1790, it was determined by Lord Cornwallis, with reference to the administration of criminal justice,* that "the future control of so important a branch of Government ought not to be left to the sole discretion of any native, or indeed of any single person whomsoever." That year is an important epoch in the history of this subject. By the regulations then passed, the powers of the Nawab Nazim passed to the Governor-General in Council, and the system of criminal justice was entirely remodelled.

Police administration in early times.

Before I proceed to explain the nature of the system then established, it will be necessary to describe the scheme of police administration which had been in force. Originally the zemindars appear to have been the persons who were responsible for † the public safety and the maintenance of the public roads.‡ There was a clause in the engagement of these landholders and farmers of land by which they were bound to keep the peace; and in the event of any robbery being committed on their respective estates or farms, to produce both the robbers and the property plundered. In 1772, however, the Foujdary jurisdiction of the zemindars was transferred to the Adawluts; for chakaran land had been resumed, and collusion was constantly proved or suspected between the perpetrators of offences and the officers who were maintained by the holders of land.

Scheme of Warren Hastings.

Accordingly a general system of police became one of the greatest wants of the country, and Mr. Hastings in 1774 divided Bengal for purposes of police into fourteen different

* Beaufort's Criminal Digest, p. 10.

† See Preamble to Regulation XXII. of 1793.

‡ See Bengal Council Legislative Proceedings, Vol. V., 1871, p. 142, Speech of the Lieutenant-Governor.

LECTURE VIII.

districts. Thannadars were appointed over them, landholders were enjoined to assist, chakaran lands were again applied to their original design; and Foujdars were appointed to apprehend all offenders against the public peace. This system proved a failure, and lasted a very few years.

Civil Judges appointed Magistrates

In 1781 the Foujdars and their subordinate thannadars were abolished, and the Judges of the Civil Courts were invested with the power, as Magistrates, of apprehending and bringing to trial offenders in their districts. Their duty was to forward them to the Darogah of the nearest Criminal Court; the power of punishment still resting with the Nabob's Court. The zemindar, by special permission of the Governor-General in Council, was sometimes vested with a similar power.

Further measures.

Subsequently the Civil Judges were vested with authority to hear and decide complaints of slight offences, and under certain restrictions to inflict corporal punishment, and impose fines on offenders. And in order to afford the Government some oversight and control over the penal jurisdiction of the country, a new office * was established at the Presidency under the immediate superintendence of the Governor-General. To this office reports of proceedings, with lists of commitments and convictions, were transmitted every month, and an officer under the Governor-General, with the title of *Remembrancer to the Criminal Courts*, was appointed for the transaction of its affairs. "But † the numerous robberies, murders, and other enormities, which continued to be daily committed throughout the country, evinced that the administration of criminal justice was in a very defective state; and as these evils appeared to result principally from the great delay which occurred in bringing offenders to punishment, and to the law not being duly enforced, as well as to other

* Regulation IX. of 1793, ss. 31, 33, and 36.

† *Ibid.*, see Preamble.

material defects in the constitution of the Criminal Courts; and as it was essential for the prevention of crimes not only that offenders should be deprived of the means of eluding the pursuit of the officers of justice, but that they should be speedily and impartially tried when apprehended, the Governor-General in Council passed certain regulations on the 3rd December, 1790, establishing Courts of Circuit under the superintendence of English Judges, assisted by Natives versed in the Mahomedan law, for trying in the first instance persons charged with crimes or misdemeanours, and enabling the Governor-General and the Members of the Supreme Council to sit in the Nizamut Adawlut (which was for that purpose again removed to Calcutta), and superintend the administration of criminal justice throughout the provinces." The regulations so passed in 1790 were, with amendments and alterations, re-enacted in 1793.

System of 1793.

Thus in 1793 the whole criminal and police administration of the country was remodelled in pursuance of previous regulations. The authority of the Nabob Nazim was abolished, and the Governor-General and Council formed the Sudder Nizamut Adawlut, having general control over the Criminal Courts.

Sudder Nizamut Adawlut.

By Regulation II. of 1801, the Court of Nizamut Adawlut, as well as that of Dewanny Adawlut, which had up to that time consisted of the Governor-General and the Members of Council, was directed to be composed of a Chief Judge and Puisne Judges; * and from that time both Courts exercised their functions distinct from the legislative and executive authority of the State. The proceedings of those Courts

* They were assisted by the head Cazee of Bengal, Behar, Orissa, and Benares. For this officer, see Reg. IX. of 1793, sec. 67, Reg. XXXIX. of 1793, and Reg. XLIX. of 1795, which extends his jurisdiction to Benares. See further Reg. VIII. of 1809, which provided for the abolition of the office of Cazee.

LECTURE VIII.

were not required from that time to be kept in English farther than the Courts might find convenient and conducive to regularity; nor were copies of the proceedings of either Court to be thereafter required, except in cases of appeal to His Majesty in Council, or of reference to the Governor-General in Council. In later years the number of Judges was increased, as in the Sudder Dewanny Adawlut.*

Courts of Circuit.

Next in rank to the Nizamut Adawlut came four Courts of Circuit, subsequently increased in number as other provinces were added to the Presidency. Each Court was composed of the same Judges who sat in the provincial Civil Court of Appeal, and of the Cazee, and Mooftee, attached thereto. The duties of the Court of Circuit, including the gaol deliveries at the principal stations, were in ordinary cases performed by the second, third, and fourth Judge, in regular succession, the first Judge remaining at the principal station, unless otherwise ordered to conduct the public business.

Abolished in 1829.

These Courts of Circuit continued to exist till the year 1829, when they were abolished by Regulation I. of that year. They were considered to have failed to afford prompt administration of justice.

Replaced by Commissioners of Revenue and Circuit.

Accordingly, in that year, Bengal was divided into twenty divisions under twenty Commissioners of Revenue and Circuit, who were entrusted with the powers formerly vested in the Courts of Circuit, together with those belonging to the Board of Revenue; the former to be exercised under the authority of the Nizamut Adawlut, the latter under the control of a Sudder Board of Revenue. The Governor-General in Council was empowered to direct any Commissioner or Judge to hold the sessions of gaol delivery for any city or zillah, with the powers and authority of any Court of Circuit. Commissioners thus became the Criminal Judges in all cases

* Reg. XII. of 1811.

of importance. Two years afterwards it was found that the labours cast upon the Commissioners were too heavy.

Criminal jurisdiction of zillah Judges.

Thereupon in the year 1831* the Magistrates were authorized to refer to the native officers, that is the Sudder Ameens, any criminal case for investigation, although such Ameens were not authorized to make any commitment. By another regulation of that year,† zillah and city Judges not being Magistrates were empowered, when ordered by the Governor-General in Council to conduct the duties of the sessions, to try commitments made by Magistrates, and to hold gaol deliveries for each district at least once in every month. Thus the Criminal Judges of the country were first the Commissioners of Division, secondly, any Civil Judge whom the Governor-General might temporarily appoint to hold sessions under the Regulation of 1829, or might generally invest with criminal jurisdiction under the Regulation of 1831.

In 1832 it was considered desirable to enable the European functionaries who presided in the Courts for the administration of criminal or civil justice, to avail themselves of the assistance of respectable natives in the decision of suits, or in the conduct of trials which might come before them. Provision was accordingly made‡ for referring suits to a panchayet, or for constituting assessors to assist the Judge, the decision however being vested exclusively in the officer presiding in Court.

Sessions Judges.

The practice which grew up under this state of the law was for the local Governments to appoint particular persons to be "District and Sessions Judges."§ There are several passages in the Regulation of 1831 and in Act VII. of 1835 which assumed the existence of such a functionary as a Sessions

* Regulation V. of 1831.

† Regulation VII. of 1831.

‡ Regulation VI. of 1832.

§ Legislative Proceedings, 1871, p. 534; Speech of Mr. Fitzjames Stephen.

LECTURE VIII.

Judge; but there was no express legislative authority for his existence, nor for the power of the local Governments to appoint him. In the Criminal Procedure Code of 1861 reference is made to a Court of Session, but in Bengal and the North-Western Provinces, the powers which the Sessions Judges assumed to exercise were derived from the old Courts of Circuit. Neither in Madras nor in Bombay were the Sessions Judges directly connected by law with the Court of Session referred to in the Code of Criminal Procedure. The practice of appointing separate persons to be District and Sessions Judges was for a long space of time utterly without authority. But it continued after the repeal in 1868 of the Regulation of 1831 and Act VII. of 1835, to which apparently it traced its existence. After that repeal the only law under which a Sessions Judge could be appointed was the Regulation of 1829, which authorized an occasional transference of a Judge to criminal work.

Bengal Sessions Courts Act of 1871.

It was under this state of things that Mr. Fitzjames Stephen introduced into the Legislative Council the Bengal Sessions Courts Act of 1871. The Act provided for the appointment of Sessions Judges and Additional Sessions Judges by the local Governments in Bengal and the North-Western Provinces. It confirmed the existing appointments, invested the Judges appointed with the character of Courts of Session within the meaning of the Code of Criminal Procedure; it authorized the Lieutenant-Governors to define and vary the local limits of their jurisdiction; it confirmed all proceedings by the existing Judges, and indemnified them against the consequences of acting without authority.

The Act was merely a temporary measure, passed in order to give a legal jurisdiction and existence to the Superior Courts of Criminal Justice which had previously been wanting. It was repealed in 1872, the Criminal Procedure Code of that year constituting all the Criminal Courts of the country.

Act of 1872.

Criminal justice in Madras.

In the Presidency of Madras a system of administration of criminal justice was introduced in 1802 during the government of Lord Clive's son, framed upon the system which prevailed in Bengal. Magistrates and Assistant Magistrates were appointed, with power to apprehend, bring to trial, and in light cases to inflict petty punishment. Four Courts of Circuit were established, and a Chief Criminal Court consisting of the Governor and Council.

The system so introduced was afterwards modified and altered. In 1827 Assistant Judges were appointed under Regulation I. of that year, and then * were constituted joint criminal Judges of their zillahs. Native criminal Judges were appointed in that year, without jurisdiction over Europeans and Americans, and were afterwards called Principal Sudder Ameens. Trial by jury was ordered to be gradually introduced.†

The Madras Courts of Circuit were abolished in 1845, and the Judges of zillah Courts were directed to hold permanent Sessions for trial of persons accused of crimes formerly triable by Courts of Circuit. Natives might be called in to assist either as assessors or as a jury.

Criminal justice in Bombay.

With regard to the Presidency of Bombay, the Governor-General in Council in 1797 authorized the local Government to establish Courts of Civil and Criminal Judicature in the Western Presidency, on principles similar to those on which the Courts in the Bengal Presidency had been established. As respects the administration of criminal justice, Mahomedan law did not generally prevail in the Presidency of Bombay. Hindus were tried by their own criminal law, Parsis and Christians by English law. Judges' and Magistrates' Courts and Courts of Session were established, and the Governor in Council had a right of supervision and control, an appellate jurisdiction and a power of granting pardon or mitigation of punishment.

* Madras Regulation II. of 1827.

† Madras Regulation X. of 1827.

LECTURE VIII.

In 1827 the Code was passed, revising former regulations, and establishing the basis of the whole judicial and police system of Bombay. Magistrates and police officers apprehended offenders and punished for slight offences. Zillah Judges and assistant zillah Judges exercised criminal jurisdiction; the Court of Circuit, held by one of the Foujdary Adawlut Judges, retaining cognizance of the most heinous crimes. A special Court was also established for the trial of political offences consisting of three Judges selected from those of the Sudder Foujdary Adawlut and the zillah Courts. All those Criminal Courts were authorized to call in the assistance of Natives, and the law which they administered was set forth in a regulation * defining offences and specifying punishments.

In 1830 the Provincial Court of Circuit was abolished, and the Criminal Judges were vested with the powers of Sessions Judges and Courts of Circuit. Joint Sessions Judges were appointed under Act XXIX. of 1845.

In 1827 appeals from the special Court for the trial of political offences which formerly lay to the Governor in Council were transferred to the Foujdary Adawlut, whose order therein was subject to the confirmation of the Government. And in 1841 it was enacted that crimes against the State should be cognizable by the ordinary tribunals.

Sudder Nizamut for the North-West Provinces.

A Court of Nizamut Adawlut was constituted for the North-West Provinces by Regulation VI. of 1831, possessing the same powers as were vested in the Nizamut Adawlut in Calcutta.

Police in Bengal.

Then, with regard to the administration of police, it was in 1793, at about the same time as the Courts of Circuit were established, placed under the exclusive charge of officers appointed to the superintendence of it on the part of Government. The landholders and farmers of land, who were

* Regulation XIV. of 1827.

Lecture VIII.

bound to keep up establishments of thannadars and police officers for the preservation of the peace, were required to discharge them, and were prohibited from entertaining such establishments in future. They were relieved of responsibility for robberies committed on their estates, unless connivance were proved, or unless they omitted to assist the police.

Supervision of police by Magistrates.

The Magistrates divided their zillahs into police jurisdictions, each of which was guarded by a Darogah or Superintendent, with an establishment of officers. The Magistrates appointed Darogahs, and were held responsible for selecting persons duly qualified for the trust. The police officers were directed to apprehend and send to the Magistrates all persons charged with crimes and misdemeanours and vagrants. The Magistrates and police officers of the cities were invested with concurrent authority in their respective jurisdictions. The cities were divided into wards, and guarded by Darogahs, who were subject to the authority of the Kutwals of each city.

Zillah Judges declared to be Magistrates.

Further, the Judges of all the zillahs and city Courts were declared to be Magistrates of the zillah or city under their respective jurisdictions, and the public gaols were placed under their charge. Shortly afterwards, assistants were appointed to the Magistrates, with a limited occasional exercise of judicial powers. In 1807 the Magistrates were given an extended jurisdiction, and in 1810 * Government was authorized to appoint other persons, not being zillah or city Judges, to exercise with them the office of Joint Magistrates. In 1818 † their jurisdiction was extended, and they were empowered to try offenders charged with burglary and theft, with a power of imprisonment for a term not exceeding two years.

Police in Benares.

Notwithstanding the introduction of this scheme of Government police, when Benares and other provinces were annexed, they were placed under the management of tehsildars,

* Regulation XVI. of 1810.
† Regulation XII. of 1818.

Lecture VIII.

landowners, and farmers, who were made responsible for robberies committed within the limits of their estates, excepting night robberies on the open roads or in woods.* But in 1807 all those provinces were divided into police jurisdictions in a similar manner to that adopted throughout Bengal, Behar, and Orissa. A superintendent of police was first appointed in 1808, and from 1816, in addition to the management of the whole system of police being entrusted to their care, they were directed by Government to submit annual reports of all the police occurrences within their districts.

Assimilated to Bengal.

Police officers.

Various rules were, from time to time, enacted respecting the duties of the Darogahs and other subordinate officers of police; and in 1817 they were all reduced into one regulation,† the whole system being revised, without, however, introducing any material alteration. The relative rank and general functions of officers on the thannah establishments were defined as follows:—The Darogahs exercised a general control over the mohurrahs, jemadars, and burkundazes attached to their respective thannahs. It was declared to be the duty of a Darogah to conform to all instructions he might receive from the magistrate, to preserve the peace within the limits of his jurisdiction, and to report to him all occurrences connected with the police, and to discover and apprehend offenders, to execute process, and obey all orders transmitted to him by the Magistrate. The Mohurrah was the second officer at the thannah, his duty being to preserve the records, and write reports, and to exercise the powers of a Darogah in the absence of that functionary. The Jemadar was the third officer, and could exercise the powers of a Darogah in the absence of both the Darogah and the Mohurrah. His duty was to see that the burkundazes were in attendance at their

Darogahs.

Mohurrahs.

Jemadars.

* Regulation XVII. of 1795, Regulation XXXV. of 1803, and Regulation IX. of 1804.

† Regulation XX. of 1817.

LECTURE VIII.

post properly armed, and that all prisoners and property brought to the thannah were duly guarded. He acted under the orders of the Darogah. The police officers generally were directed to obey the orders of the superintendents of police and of the Joint and Assistant Magistrates. Village watchmen were directed to be employed within the limits of the authority of the Darogahs, and to be subject to their orders. In those towns and villages where Darogahs were stationed, the duties of watching were performed jointly by the police officers and the village watchmen. The kutwals and police officers in cities and towns were to be guided by the regulation, so far as it was applicable to them.

Watchers.

Control by Commissioners of Circuit.

In 1829, when the Courts of Circuit were abolished, the magistracy and the police were placed under the superintendence and control of Commissioners of Circuit, who replaced those Courts and succeeded to their powers. The office of superintendent of police was at the same time abolished,* and its duties were assumed by the Commissioners. In 1837, however, provision was made for re-appointing superintendents of police, who thereupon were empowered to exercise the functions of the Commissioners.

Police in Madras.

No general system of police was introduced into Madras when the system of Criminal Administration was first established. The Native system was retained; village watchers everywhere existing under the superintendence of the headmen of the villages. In some places Darogahs and thannadars were appointed.

But in 1816 a regulation† was passed to organize a general system throughout the Presidency. Heads of villages, aided by village watchers, were to discharge the duties of policemen, *i.e.* except in trivial cases, arrest and forward accused persons to the tehsildar or police officer of the district.

* Regulation I. of 1829.

† Regulation XI. of 1816.

LECTURE VIII.

The tehsildar was the head of the police of the district. Zemindars could be invested with police authority. The Magistrates and their assistants were generally charged with the maintenance of peace.

Police in Bombay.

At the same time, a general system of police was established throughout the territories subject to the Bombay Government, by which the duties of police, which had originally been confided to the Foujdars and thannadars, were transferred to the heads of villages, aided by watchers. The new system was framed on the same plan as that adopted in Madras in 1816. In 1820, a Sudder Foujdary Adawlut was established at Surat consisting of four Judges, empowered to take cognizance of all matters relating to criminal justice and the police, and to call for the proceedings of the Criminal Judges or zillah Magistrates. The Judges were directed to go on circuit.

By the Revised Code in 1827, the duties of the police were directed to be conducted by the Judge and Collector of each zillah, the district police officer, and the heads of villages. The Magistrates and their assistants were empowered to apprehend all persons charged with crimes or offences.

General condition of the Police.

About the middle of this century the general condition of the police throughout the country attracted considerable attention from the Government.

For upwards of half a century, the Magistrate had been charged with the oversight of the police of his district; and as with the increase of business, Magistrates became judicial officers, with extended powers, they were little able to give the police the attention necessary to keep it efficient. Complaints* of their inefficiency and corruption became universal.

* About the time of Lord Wm. Bentinck. See for an historical account of the Indian Police, the speech of Sir B. Frere introducing Act V. of 1861 to the Legislative Council of India, from which this *résumé* is taken.

Whether few or many in proportion to the population, the police was everywhere oppressive and corrupt, undisciplined and ill-supervised. The Magistrates were either inefficient superintendents of police, or if active as police officers, apt to be biassed as Magistrates. The earliest attempts at reform were made in the Presidency Towns by appointing superintendents of police separate from the Magistrate, and appointing non-official Justices of the Peace, Native and European. The result everywhere demonstrated the soundness of the principle of the separation, whilst the Justices of the Peace discharged the duties entrusted to them in a very satisfactory manner.

Sir Charles Napier's reform of it in Sind.

The first real attempt to reform the Mofussil police was made in Sind by Sir Charles Napier. Immediately after the conquest of that province, he drew up a plan on the model of the Irish constabulary, of which the characteristics were separate organization, complete severance of police and judicial functions, complete subordination to the general government, and lastly, discipline, not in the nature of parade, but as far as was necessary to effective organization. Its introduction was received with great distrust by the civil officers, but the total suppression of organized violent crime which ensued, and the conduct and efficiency of the Sind police during the Mutiny, testified to the soundness of the measure.

N.W. Provinces.

Lord Ellenborough ordered its extension to the North-Western Provinces, and three police corps were raised to relieve the military of the civil duties previously performed by them. Lord Ellenborough, however, left India, and there the reform stopped.

Bombay and Punjab.

In 1847, Sir George Clerk, Governor of Bombay, visited Sind, and recognizing the value of the Sind police, commenced reforms on a similar principle in Bombay, and shortly afterwards Sir Henry Lawrence commenced the re-organization of the police of the Punjab on much the same plan.

Lecture VIII.

The original plan was, however, departed from in many particulars, and a double system of police was created, *viz.* first, the employment of an unorganized body of burkundazes under the Deputy Commissioners as Magistrates; and, secondly, the formation of police corps under the Chief Commissioner, who did no real police work, but were employed on duties which had previously devolved on the regular army. The system, although very costly, was effective, and it was these police corps which so materially assisted Sir John Lawrence to hold the Punjab and retake Delhi. This Punjab police was the model for the police corps of the North-Western Provinces since 1857, and also for the police corps which existed in Oudh before the Mutiny.

Oudh.

In March, 1858, Colonel Bruce submitted, by order of Sir R. Montgomery, a scheme on the Sind model for the police of Oudh, and raised a police force to aid in subduing the country. Three thousand cavalry and twelve thousand infantry took the field with Lord Clyde in 1858, and occupied the country as the army passed over it; and in 1859, the country being thoroughly subdued, Sir Robert Montgomery decided to make the police a purely civil body, separate from the military on the one hand, and from the judiciary on the other. This was done, and a constabulary organized for Lucknow on the model of the London police. The success of the measure was great and tranquillity complete, and great reductions were made in the extent and expenditure of the police and tehsil establishments.

Madras.

Attention was first drawn to the subject of police reform in Madras by the report of the Torture Commission, and the result was embodied in the Act passed by the Legislative Council in 1859. The Act had proved most successful in operation, and it struck at the root of one of the great curses of the country, the detention by the police of persons charged with offences often without warrant and for corrupt purposes.

In August, 1860, a Police Commission was appointed in order to secure economy and something like uniformity in matters connected with police. Their report was followed by a Bill being brought into the Legislative Council which subsequently became Act V. of 1861.

Lecture VIII.

Act V. of 1861.

Its object was to provide for the reorganization and regulation of police throughout India, that is to say, in every place to which the Governor-General should by order extend its provisions. Under it the entire police establishment under a local Government is enrolled as one police force; constitituted and paid according to the order of the local Government. The local Government superintend it, while its administration in each general police district is vested in an Inspector-General and his subordinate officers; and throughout the local jurisdiction of the Magistrate of a district it is vested in a District Superintendent and his subordinates, subject to the general control and direction of the Magistrate. The chief police officers may be invested with the powers of a Magistrate. Special police officers may be appointed for such time and within such limits as the Magistrate may think necessary.

The Act does not in any way interfere with the position and privileges of any hereditary or other village police officers, unless such officer shall be enrolled as a police officer under the Act, which cannot be done without his consent.

The duty of a police officer is promptly to obey and execute all orders and warrants lawfully issued to him by any competent authority; to collect and communicate intelligence affecting the public peace; to prevent the commission of offences and public nuisances; to detect and bring offenders to justice; and to apprehend all persons whom he is legally authorized to apprehend, and for whose apprehension sufficient ground exists.

THE EXISTING JUDICIAL SYSTEM.

LECTURE IX.

THE PRIVY COUNCIL.

Introduction—History of the Privy Council—Growth of its authority—Struggles to repress it—Its extravagant powers under the Tudors—First exercise of appellate jurisdiction over the Colonies—Loss of jurisdiction in England—Nature of the present jurisdiction—Appeals from India—From the Supreme Court—From Bengal Sudder Court—From Madras and Bombay Sudder Courts—Fate of appeals—Power of the Council to entertain appeals—Limited by Legislation—And by Charters—No appeals in cases of felony—Act of William the Fourth—Acts of the Governor-General in Council—Charters of the High Court.

Introduction. I HAVE now completed the history of the Courts and legislative authorities in India and have described the existing Legislatures. An account of the existing judicial system at present established and in force will complete the subject under discussion.

The highest judicial authority enforced in India, to which all its Courts are ultimately subordinate, is that of Her Majesty in Council, in pursuance of judgments delivered by the Privy Council. Although that tribunal sits in London and exercises supreme appellate authority over other Courts than those established in India, *viz.*, the Courts of the Colonies and the Ecclesiastical Courts in England, yet some account of it is necessary to give a complete view of the Indian system.

History of the Privy Council. It would require a very minute examination of English history to explain how the Sovereign as represented by the Privy Council on the one hand, and the House of Lords as a distinct branch of the Legislature on the other, became possessed of their respective jurisdictions, dividing between them the ultimate control over the administration of justice. In general terms, however, I may give a brief outline of that history, as it will explain the circumstance of India being subject in respect of the ultimate appellate jurisdiction over it to the Sovereign in Council rather than to the House of Lords.

For a long period* in the early history of England, there was a great Council or Parliament on the one side, and a select Council which surrounded the King on the other. Legislative and judicial rights belonged to the larger assembly, but were constantly exercised by the smaller Council, who in matters of high importance convened the larger assembly in order to give greater stability to their acts. The assembling of the larger Council, however, gradually fell into disuse. And the fate of judicial authority was chiefly determined by the strong rivalry which grew up between the secular and ecclesiastical powers for the possession of separate and then superior jurisdiction.

Towards the close of the 12th century, the three superior Courts of Common Law, with purely secular jurisdiction, were established. As they became more independent and distinct, the Privy Council, although it inherited strong claims to appellate jurisdiction, and a power by virtue of Royal prerogative and early precedent to interfere with the proceedings of the Courts, was obliged to abstain from violating their independence. The Council represented the authority of Government, from which an insecure state of society required a constant interference. The Courts, on the other hand, derived their strength from that passionate attachment to law which animated the Saxon people, and which inspired unceasing efforts to render that law supreme over the Executive.

* I condense this account from a paper contributed by me to the *Calcutta Review* in 1862.

LECTURE IX.

Growth of its authority.

The Wars of the Roses increased the disorders of society, and thereby ultimately strengthened the power of the Executive by multiplying the occasions for its interference. During that period the Privy Council increased its authority. Besides the establishment of the three Courts of Common Law, there arose the Court of Chancery, with an extensive equitable jurisdiction mostly exercised by Ecclesiastical Chancellors, and a right to interfere with the course of law. The Council and the Court of Chancery were for a long period closely connected. The original bond of union was in the person of the Chancellor, who presided in both, and from whom the process of each originated. According to Sir Francis Palgrave,* for a considerable period the Chancellor never exercised any judicial functions, unless when directed by the Council or acting by its authority.

Struggles to repress it.

Finally, however, at the end of the 14th century, the Court of Chancery gained exclusive cognizance over trusts and all fiduciary relations, and established its independence of the Privy Council. Further than that, the great Council of older times developed into a Parliament, and the House of Lords endeavoured to reconstitute themselves the High Court of English justice. The Commons also aspired to share in the supreme judicial authority, and instances are recorded of their interference. From the time of the establishment of Parliament, statutes were constantly made which were aimed at the authority of the Council, and directed to vindicate the right of the free man to the judgment of his peers and to the due course of law. The growth, therefore, of Parliament, of Chancery, and of the Courts of Common Law tended strongly to restrict the authority of the Council to the discharge of purely executive functions, and to reduce the jurisdiction of its members to the narrowest limits. Its proceedings were constantly

* Palgrave's Essay on King's Council, p. 25.

watched by Parliament, and until the long Wars of the Roses had weakened the power of resistance, the authority of the Council remained under strict control.

Its extravagant powers under the Tudors.

With the rise of the Tudors, the Council, under the name of the Star Chamber, assumed a power of adjudicating in all causes that might, in example or consequence, concern the state of the commonwealth. To use the words of Lord Bacon, "as the Chancery had the prætorian power of equity, so the Star Chamber had the censorian power for offences under the degree of capital." The erection of this Chamber was a reactionary movement against the more feudal principle which regarded the House of Lords as the supreme judicial tribunal. The arbitrary policy of the Tudor princes, and the long intermission of Parliaments during the reigns of Henry VIII. and Elizabeth, favoured the transfer of its powers to the committee of the Privy Council which sat in the Starred Chamber. In point of fact, the Council, notwithstanding all the opposition it had experienced under the Lancastrian kings, had at this time achieved a most unconstitutional triumph over the House of Lords.

First exercise of appellate jurisdiction over the Colonies.

It was at this time, *viz.*, under the Tudor princes, that the Council drew into its own hands, and never afterwards lost, the exclusive adjudication of appeals from foreign and colonial dependencies of the Crown and from the Channel Islands. It appears that appeals were first granted from Jersey in Henry VIII.'s reign, and the records of the Privy Council in 1572 present the first instance of the exercise of this jurisdiction. The jurisdiction of the House of Lords had at this time fallen into disuse, partly from the intrinsic decay of the peerage, and partly from the frequent intermission of Parliaments.

Loss of jurisdiction in England.

Finally, however, the atrocities of the Star Chamber roused a spirit of resistance, and occasioned a full enquiry into the position and authority of the Council. The Act of 16 Charles

LECTURE IX.

I, c. 10, abolished the Star Chamber and the whole of its cognate jurisdiction, and, notwithstanding four centuries of possession and established right, the civil jurisdiction of the Privy Council was declared to be a usurpation contrary to the laws of the land. The fervid loyalty of 1660, notwithstanding all the excesses in which it indulged, was unable to efface the strong hatred produced by the acts of the Star Chamber, or to restore to the Privy Council either its equity or criminal jurisdiction in England.

No question respecting the jurisdiction of the Council survived the revolution of 1688, but the narrow bounds within which it has been restrained are a striking contrast to the whole of its previous career. The only relic of its ancient criminal jurisdiction is its right to examine and commit for high treason, but the power of punishment has entirely passed from its hands. It still issues proclamations and is called upon to meet extraordinary emergencies, and it reserves to itself the right of granting charters. These, together with its civil jurisdiction over India and the colonies, and its right to entertain appeals from the Ecclesiastical* Courts in England, alone remain of its former judicial authority. The result is that the House of Lords has regained since the Restoration the whole of the appellate jurisdiction over the English Courts of law and equity. The functions of the House of Lords are, however, according to established usage exercised by a Committee of Law-lords, with whom sit since the Judicature Acts the Lords of Appeal in Ordinary; and the functions of the Privy Council are exercised by a Judicial Committee

* See the Supreme Court of Judicature Acts, 1873 and 1875. Appeals from the Admiralty Courts in England lay to the Privy Council from 1833 until 1876, when they were transferred to the new Court of Appeal. Previously to 1833 (see 2 & 3 Will. IV. c. 92) both ecclesiastical and maritime appeals lay to the High Court of Delegates, under Acts of Henry VIII. and Elizabeth.

established by the Act of William IV.* The only practical result is that a division of labour is effected, since under existing circumstances no constitutional principle can be said to be involved in the exclusive retention by either body of its particular jurisdiction.

The extent and importance of the jurisdiction still retained by the Privy Council were pointed out by Lord Brougham† in his celebrated speech on Law Reform in 1828:—

Nature of the present jurisdiction.

"They determine," he said, "not only upon questions of colonial law in plantation cases, but also sit as Judges, in the last resort, of all prize causes. And they hear and decide upon all our plantation appeals. They are thus made the supreme Judges, in the last resort, over every one of our foreign settlements, whether situated in those immense territories which you possess in the East, where you and a trading company rule together over not less than 70,000,000 of subjects—or established among those rich and populous islands which stud the Indian Ocean and form the Great Eastern Archipelago—or have their stations in those lands part lying within the tropics, part stretching towards the pole, peopled by various castes, differing widely in habits, still more widely in privileges, great in numbers, abounding in wealth, extremely unsettled in their notions of right, and excessively litigious, as all the children of the new world are supposed to be, both from their physical and political constitution. All this immense jurisdiction over the rights of property and person, over rights political and legal, and over all the questions growing out of so vast and varied a province, is exercised by the Privy Council unaided and alone. It is obvious that, from the mere distance of those colonies and the immense variety of matters arising in them, foreign to our habits and

* 3 & 4 Will. IV. c. 41.

† Lord Brougham's Speeches, Vol. II., p. 356.

LECTURE IX.

beyond the scope of our knowledge, any judicial tribunal in this country must of necessity be an extremely inadequate Court of Review. But what adds incredibly to the difficulty is that hardly any two of the colonies can be named which have the same law; and, in the greater number, the law is wholly unlike our own. In some settlements it is the Dutch law, in others the Spanish, in others the French, in others the Danish. In our Eastern possessions these variations are, if possible, greater;—while one territory is swayed by the Mahomedan law, another is ruled by the Hindu law; and this, again, in some of our possessions is qualified or superseded by the law of Buddha: the English jurisprudence being confined to the handful of British settlers and the inhabitants of the three Presidencies."

Appeals from India.

The first occasion upon which a right of appeal was granted by Royal Charter to the Privy Council from the judgments of the Courts in India was in 1726. The Charter granted by George I. in that year established the Mayors' Courts in the three Presidencies, and gave a right of appeal from those Courts, first to the Governors in Council and thence to the Privy Council, where the amount in dispute exceeded the sum of 1000 pagodas, *i.e.* 4000 rupees. Both the Act of Parliament and the Charter to which the Supreme Court of Bengal owed its existence reserved a similar right of appeal to the Sovereign in Council. The same right was also reserved in reference to the Recorders' Courts and the Supreme Courts at Madras and Bombay. Any person aggrieved by a decision of any of those Courts in a suit the value of which was over 1000 pagodas (except in the case of the Supreme Court of Bombay, where the value of the suit must have been above 3000 Bombay rupees) could petition the Sovereign in Council, and the Council was empowered to refuse or to admit the appeal and to reform, correct, or vary such decision, according to the Royal pleasure.

From the Supreme Court.

Such were the regulations with regard to Courts established by Royal Charter. In 1781, on the establishment of the Sudder Court of Bengal, an appeal was given from its decisions in civil suits the value of which should be of £5000 and upwards. No rules were prescribed by Parliament respecting the appeals so authorized. Rules and orders were framed by the Supreme Court and approved by His Majesty in Council according to the provisions of the Charter which established that Court. No such power was given by Act of Parliament to the Sudder Court, and consequently Regulation XVI. of 1797 was passed in order to provide rules relative to appeals to the Privy Council against decisions of that Court until the King's pleasure should be known thereupon. That regulation limited the right of appeal in point of time to a period of six months from the date of the judgment, and in point of value to cases where the judgment exclusive of costs of suit was of the value of Rs. 50,000. *From Bengal Sudder Court.*

In 1818, the right of appeal from the Sudder Courts of Madras and Bombay to the Privy Council was established, and in all the Presidencies reservation was made of the Sovereign's right to reject or receive appeals notwithstanding any provisions in the regulations for the purpose of limiting or controlling the exercise of the right of appeal. *From Madras and Bombay Sudder Courts.*

It appears that in the sixty years which elapsed from the establishment of the Supreme Court of Calcutta to the Statute of William IV. which constituted the Judicial Committee of the Privy Council, only fifty appeals were instituted. The majority of those appear to have been from the Supreme Courts, which from the first were looked upon as offshoots from the Courts of Westminster Hall, the suits in them being carried on by English counsel and attorneys and the suitors in them being either Europeans or Natives in the habit of close intercourse with Europeans. Both the suitors and practitioners in the provincial Courts were very little acquainted *Fate of appeals.*

with the mode of procedure in appeals to England, and either shrank from the attempt to prosecute such appeals, or from total ignorance as to the necessary proceedings failed either to follow up or to withdraw any appeal which had been commenced.*

When appeals lay to the Governor-General from the different Sudder Courts, decisions had been returned without anything being required to be done by the parties; consequently when appeal cases were transmitted to England, the parties patiently waited for a decision, but in vain, and in many cases the property in dispute was eaten up by private and public debt, and the litigants were either ruined or greatly impoverished.

Power of the Council to entertain appeals.

With regard to the power of the Council to entertain appeals and the right of the suitor to prefer them, the general principle is that † the Crown has an inherent general right controlled by Acts of Parliament to admit appeals from its subjects beyond the seas; but that Orders in Council and local rules are intended to regulate the manner in which that right shall be exercised.

In some cases it has been considered not only that local rules or general principles do not authorize an appeal (either because the order is not properly appealable, or because the due course has not been followed by the parties), but that they prevent the Privy Council from exercising any discretion in advising the Crown as to admitting one. In other cases, that although an appeal cannot be brought as of right, yet the Privy Council are not precluded from the exercise of their discretion upon the subject.‡

Limited by legislation.

A petition for leave to appeal,§ where the sum in dispute

* Morley's Administration of Justice in India, pp. 145—8.

† Macpherson's Judicial Committee Practice, p. 1.

‡ *Ibid.*, p. 4.

§ Cuvillier *v.* Aylwin, 2 Knapp, p. 72, decided in 1832.

was of less amount than £500 sterling, was disallowed by the Privy Council, because the Colonial Legislature, in pursuance of powers conferred by the Imperial Parliament, had by its provisions on the subject of appeals deprived the subject of his right to appeal. LECTURE IX.

Again, appeals might have been brought with the leave of the Supreme Courts in India from their decisions in criminal cases; but upon the principle of the case just stated, it was held that, as the Charter of the Supreme Court of Bombay was granted by the Crown in pursuance of an Act of Parliament, the Crown, authorized by statute, had thereby abandoned its prerogative to receive appeals in cases of felony, except upon leave obtained from the Court below.* And by Charters

In another† case, Lord Brougham observed, in delivering the judgment of the Privy Council, that even independently of the statute "it might be reasonably contended that the Crown may point out the manner in which the general common law right of appeal to it from colonial sentences shall be exercised by a particular mode of enactment in the Charter. It may say there is a right to appeal to the Crown generally. That appeal shall be in civil cases at all times, but shall be in criminal cases only in a certain manner and form, and I shall delegate to my Judges below the right to refuse or to grant it, as they see fit."

And in the former* case cited, Dr. Lushington remarked, "not only in England, but throughout the dominions of the Crown of Great Britain, governed by the law of England, no right of appeal in felonies has ever existed. Nor are we aware that in any one single instance the Crown has ever, by the exercise of its prerogative, granted leave to appeal in any such case." No appeal in cases of felony.

It was therefore fully settled that in cases of felony, when the

* Queen *v.* Edaljee Byramjee, 5 Moore P. C. 272.

† Queen *v.* Alloo Paroo, 5 Moore P. C. 296.

LECTURE IX.

Supreme Court of Bombay or any of the Supreme Courts of India had not granted leave to appeal, the Privy Council could not grant or advise the Crown to grant such leave, whether the appeal were from the verdict and judgment, or were confined to matter of error appearing upon the record. The Court below alone had the power of granting or refusing any appeal in such cases.

Act of William the Fourth.

In 1833, the Act 3 & 4 William IV. c. 41, was passed, and under it a permanent Judicial Committee was appointed for the disposal of appeals and other matters referred to them by His Majesty in Council in pursuance of the Act. The Committee was composed of the President of the Council and the Lord Chancellor, and several of the Judges of highest rank in the kingdom, with power to the Sovereign to add any two Privy Councillors as members of the Committee. Exclusive power was given to it to review all sentences of Courts abroad which were formerly appealable to the High Court of Admiralty or to the Commissioners in prize cases in England. In addition to that the entire appellate jurisdiction of the Sovereign in Council was directed to be exercised solely by the Judicial Committee; and power was given to the Crown to refer to the Committee for hearing or consideration "any such other matters whatsoever as His Majesty should think fit," in order that they should advise the Crown thereon. Four members, and, since 1843, three members* of the Committee form a quorum, a majority of whom must concur in their report or recommendation. The Crown was empowered to require the attendance at the committee for the purposes of the Act of any Privy Councillor who should be a Judge of one of the three superior Courts of Common Law.

They have power to examine or direct the examination of witnesses at discretion; to remit the cause to the Court

* See 6 & 7 Vict. c. 38, s. 1.

below for rehearing, either generally or with respect to certain points; and upon such rehearing to take further evidence, to admit evidence before rejected or reject evidence before admitted, and to direct issues to be tried in any Court in Her Majesty's dominions abroad. LECTURE IX.

All appeals were directed to be made within the time fixed by any existing law or usage, or within such time as should be ordered by the Council. Then with regard to the pending appeals (where there had been a delay of two years from the date of their admission) from the Sudder Dewanny Adawlut in the East Indies, the Act recited that transcripts of the proceedings had been received, but that the suitors had not duly prosecuted the same to a hearing, and thereupon it empowered the Sovereign in Council to give such directions to the East India Company and other persons as should be thought necessary for the purpose of bringing those appeals to a hearing.

In 1838 an Order in Council was issued which limited appeals from the Supreme Courts in India in point of time to six months from the date of the judgment and in point of value to Rs. 10,000 instead of Rs. 50,000.

As soon as the old appeals from the Sudder Courts in India had been determined, an Act was passed* which provided that from the commencement of the year 1846, all appeals admitted by the Sudder Courts should be taken to be abandoned and withdrawn by consent of the parties thereto unless some proceedings therein should be taken in England within two years after the arrival of the transcript.

Acts of the Governor-General in Council.

In 1863† an Act was passed to regulate the admission of appeals to Her Majesty in Council from certain judgments and orders not subject to the general regulations; but this

* 8 & 9 Vict. c. 30.
† Act II. of 1863.

LECTURE IX.

was repealed by Act VI. of 1874, which consolidated and amended the law upon the subject. This Act was itself repealed and then re-enacted word for word by Act. X. of 1877, and then by Act XIV. of 1882 (the Code of Civil Procedure), sections 594 to 616. Appeals are directed to lie to Her Majesty in Council from any final decree passed by the High Court or any other Court of final appellate jurisdiction in all cases where the amount or value of the matter directly or indirectly in dispute is 10,000 rupees or upwards; but where the decree appealed from affirms the decision of the Court immediately below it, the appeal to Her Majesty must involve some substantial question of law. In other cases an appeal only lies when it is certified to be a case fit for appeal. Nothing, however, in the Act is to bar the unqualified exercise of Her Majesty's pleasure, or to interfere with the rules made by the Judicial Committee.

Charters of the High Courts.

The Charters of the High Courts give a right of appeal to suitors in any matter not being of criminal jurisdiction from any final judgment, decree or order of those Courts made on appeal, or in the exercise of original jurisdiction by a majority of the full number of Judges, or of any Division Court from which an appeal does not lie to the High Court itself. The right so conferred is subject to the proviso that the matter in dispute is of the value of not less than Rs. 10,000, or that such judgment, decree or order involves directly or indirectly some claim to property of that value. An appeal also lies from any other final judgment, decree or order when the High Court shall declare that the case is a fit one for appeal.

The High Courts under the Charter may grant leave to appeal to the Privy Council from any preliminary or interlocutory judgment, decree or order, or sentences in any matter not being of criminal jurisdiction.

Further, a power of appeal is given (provided the High

Court declares the case is a fit one for such appeal and under such conditions as it may require) from any judgment, order or sentence of the High Court made in the exercise of original criminal jurisdiction, or in any criminal case where any point or points of law have been reserved for the opinion of the High Court.

The High Court is directed by its Charter in all cases of appeal to certify and transmit to the Privy Council a copy of the proceedings so far as they relate to the appeal, and of the reasons given by the Judges for or against the judgment appealed against. The High Courts are also bound to execute the judgments and orders of the Privy Council.

LECTURE X.

THE SUPERIOR COURTS.

Separation between Courts of Presidency Town and Mofussil—In laws and procedure—First attempts to amalgamate them—Abolition of Supreme Courts—Bill introduced to establish High Courts—Indian High Courts Act—Charters of High Courts—Civil jurisdiction of Bengal High Court—Original—Extraordinary original—Appellate—Criminal—Testamentary and intestate—Matrimonial—Madras and Bombay High Courts—North-West Provinces—Result of the establishment of High Courts—Punjab Chief Court—Retention of the old Presidency Town system—Insolvency Courts—Insolvency jurisdiction in the Mofussil—Vice-Admiralty Courts—Divorce Courts.

Separation between Courts of Presidency Town and Mofussil.

HITHERTO I have endeavoured to trace the history of the judicial institutions which were established in the Presidency Towns and Mofussil, to account for their wide separation, their dissimilar origin, their long retention, and the very slight tendency towards amalgamation which they had exhibited. The inconveniences of such double system were numerous, but the differences in the procedure observed, and in the laws administered by these rival institutions, as well as the existence of a strong party feeling in favour of maintaining tribunals which should exercise exclusive jurisdiction over Europeans, rendered such system extremely difficult to abolish.

In laws and procedure.

With regard to the laws administered, the Courts established by the Crown and Parliament for the most part applied English law, both civil and criminal; exceptions being made in favour of Hindus and Mahomedans, that in suits against parties of either of those religions, by whomsoever they might be brought, whether by Europeans or Natives, the law of the defendant should prevail. Their proceedings also were governed by the English law of procedure. Until 1834 they for the most part were amenable only to the legislative authority of Parliament, and to such regulations of Government as the Supreme Courts might choose to acknowledge and register.

The Mofussil Courts, on the other hand, had nothing to do with English law, but were amenable in all respects to the regulations of Government; and when Hindu or Mahomedan law did not apply, or when no regulations were applicable, were directed to proceed according to justice, equity, and good conscience. That is to say, in cases for which no law was provided, the Judges were authorized to use the best discretion they possessed. Originally the number of cases for which no specific law existed must have been considerable. For, setting aside Hindu and Mahomedan law, there was no law of contract, no law of succession, no territorial law, no law of evidence, no law of administration of deceased estates. The wide field, from which all specific law was absent, was gradually reclaimed, as it were, and brought within the limits of civilization. But the process was very gradual, and until the establishment of the Indian Law Commission and the Imperial Legislature in 1834, could hardly be said even to have commenced. From that date, however, it proceeded very slowly, and it is only since 1858 that serious and effective progress has been made.

The procedure of those Courts was such as was from time to time prescribed by the regulations, which, by the constant process of repeal and amendment, at last gave a very uncertain and obscure expression to the rules which they provided.

Before the work of amalgamating these two rival sets of judicial institutions could possibly be proceeded with, it was

LECTURE X.

First attempts to amalgamate them.

absolutely necessary to make some attempts to bridge over the wide gulf which separated the laws which they respectively administered, and the procedure which they respectively observed. The abolition of the East India Company, the assumption of direct responsibility of government by the English Crown, and the consolidation of the Indian Empire under the Queen, which occurred in 1858, favoured the work of amalgamation which the influences of a century had impeded and prevented. Policy suggested that in re-establishing and consolidating the new empire something more was required than an imperial army, government, and legislature. A uniform criminal law, a uniform system of Courts of civil and criminal procedure, and in the end a uniform civil law, so far as exclusive rights to personal laws, based upon religion, would permit, and as far as practicable, equal liability to the jurisdiction, were required as a basis upon which to found a just as well as an imperial administration.

In the next three years after the proclamation of the Queen, first the Civil Procedure Code, and then the Penal Code, and almost immediately afterwards the Criminal Procedure Code, all of which had been long in preparation, were enacted. They applied to the whole empire, and all Courts were governed by the procedures therein laid down, except the Supreme Courts and those established by Royal Charter.

Abolition of Supreme Courts.

When these Codes had been passed, a very long stride had been made in the direction of one uniform system for the administration of justice in India. The next step was to abolish the Supreme Courts in the three Presidencies and the anomalous procedure observed in them, and constitute in each Presidency town a High Court of Judicature, which should be supreme over all the Courts both in the Presidency Towns and also in the Mofussil. The plan had long been in contemplation; in fact the continued existence of the Supreme

Courts, alien as they were from the rest of the judicial system, was due to the high character they had maintained, and the confidence which was reposed in them by the public, and to the divergence in law and procedure to which I have referred and to the long delays in maturing and passing the three Codes mentioned above.

LECTURE X.

Bill introduced to establish High Courts.

Those three Codes were passed respectively in the years 1859, 1860, and 1861, and in the last of those three years a Bill was introduced into Parliament for the establishment of the High Courts. As far back as 1852-53, in the evidence which was given before the Committee which sat on East Indian affairs, a strong opinion was expressed by those most competent to give it, that it was desirable with a view to the better administration of justice in India that the Supreme and Sudder Courts should, in each Presidency, be consolidated into one, so as (in the stereotyped phraseology) to unite the legal training of the English lawyers with the intimate knowledge of the customs, habits, and laws of the Natives possessed by the Judges in the country.

When Sir Charles Wood introduced the Bill in 1853, he was anxious to include a provision for effecting that object, and to empower Her Majesty to issue her Charter for the establishment of a united Court. But the members of the Indian Law Commission, though they approved of the proposed change, thought that it would be useless to attempt to unite the Courts till the Codes of Procedure were established. A Royal Commission, however, was issued to obtain the basis on which the forms of procedure could be framed.

It is worth while to observe that Sir Charles Wood, in introducing the Bill of 1861 into the House of Commons, laid special stress on the advantage of the Judges of the new* Courts going on circuit to try criminal cases. He said, "We shall have one Supreme Court, one sole Court of Appeal

* Hansard, 1861, p. 647.

Lecture X.

instead of two; and, inasmuch as the administration of justice in the minor Courts depends on the mode in which the appeals sent up from them are treated, the superior Court, thus constituted, will, I hope, improve the administration of justice generally throughout India. It is notorious that the greatest confidence is felt by the Natives in the administration of justice by the Supreme Court even at present. Now, according to the provisions of this Bill, the Judges of the Supreme Court may be sent on circuit throughout the country. The effect of this will be that in important cases occurring in the various districts, justice, as in this country, will be administered on the spot by a trained Judge. At present, if an Englishman commits a crime which may subject him to serious punishment, he and all the witnesses must be brought to Calcutta, and the case must be tried there. In future an English Judge going into the country will be able to try these cases. At present, when a crime is committed up-country by a European, the necessity of bringing him to Calcutta amounts in many cases to an absolute denial of justice. It may be impossible in a country like India to bring justice to every man's door, but at all events the system now proposed will bring it far nearer than at present; and when criminal offences are committed by a European—happily such instances are rare—the impartial administration of justice on the spot will produce a most desirable influence on the minds of the Natives.

Indian High Courts Act.

The Act was speedily passed, and by it the Crown* was empowered to establish, by Letters Patent, a High Court for the Bengal division of the Presidency of Fort William and also at Madras and Bombay; and it was enacted that thereupon the Supreme Courts and the Courts of Sudder Dewanny Adawlut and Sudder Nizamut or Foujdary Adawlut should be abolished. The jurisdiction and powers of the High Courts

* 24 & 25 Vict. c. 104.

were to be fixed by the Letters Patent. The Crown was also empowered to establish a High Court in the North-Western Provinces. Lecture X.

Thereupon Charters were issued in 1862, and afterwards new Charters in 1865, constituting the High Courts in Bengal, Madras, and Bombay. Charters of High Courts.

That in Bengal was vested with ordinary original civil jurisdiction within the local limits of Calcutta, or within such local limits as might from time to time be prescribed by competent legislative authority for India.* Suits of every description were brought within their cognizance, except cases in which the Small Cause Court would have jurisdiction and in which the debt or damage or value of the property sued for did not exceed Rs. 100. The circumstance necessary to give jurisdiction is that the land must be situated, or the cause of action must have arisen, or the defendant must, at the time of the commencement of the suit, dwell or carry on business, or personally work for gain within the local limits of Calcutta. If only part of the cause of action were within those limits, then the leave of the Court must be obtained before the institution of the suit. It has been held † that, if part of the land was situated within, and part without, the local limits, the High Court would nevertheless have jurisdiction. Civil jurisdiction of Bengal High Court. Original.

Its extraordinary original jurisdiction enables the Court to remove and to try and determine any suit falling within the jurisdiction of any Court, subject to its superintendence, whether within or without the Bengal division of the Presidency, either on the agreement of the parties to that effect or Extraordinary original.

* 28 & 29 Vict. c. 15, ss. 3—6, gave the Governor-General in Council power to alter the local limits.

† Prasannamayi Dasi *v.* Kadambini Dasi, 3 B. L. R. (O. J.), 85, Norman, J. On appeal before Peacock, C. J., and Markby, J., the question of jurisdiction was not disputed.

for purposes of justice, the reasons for so doing being recorded on its proceedings. Several causes of action between the same parties not being for land or other immovable property may be joined together in one suit and tried by the High Court if any one of those causes of action is within the High Court's jurisdiction.

Appellate.

The High Court of Bengal was also constituted a Court of Appeal from the Civil Courts of the Bengal division of the Presidency and from all other Courts subject to its superintendence. It also has the like power and authority with respect to the persons and estates of infants, idiots, and lunatics, whether within or without the Bengal division of the Presidency, as was formerly vested in the Supreme Court.

Criminal.

Its criminal jurisdiction is in respect of all persons within and without the limits of the Bengal division, and not within the limits of the criminal jurisdiction of any other Court and over whom the Supreme Court formerly had jurisdiction. It also has extraordinary original criminal jurisdiction over all persons who reside in places within the jurisdiction of any Court formerly subject to the superintendence of the Sudder Nizamut Adawlut in Calcutta upon any charge preferred by the Advocate-General or by any Magistrate or other officer specially empowered by the Government on their behalf. It is also constituted a Court of Appeal from the Criminal Courts of the Bengal division of the Presidency and from all other Courts subject to its superintendence. It is also a Court of reference and revision from the Criminal Courts subject to its appellate jurisdiction.

Testamentary and intestate.

It also succeeded to the powers of the late Supreme Court in relation to the granting of probates of last wills and testaments and letters of administration of the goods and all other effects whatsoever of deceased persons, whether within or without the Bengal division of the Presidency, except such as are within the limits of the jurisdiction for that purpose of any other High Court. It also has jurisdiction of this character under the Indian Succession Act (X. of 1865) and Act V. of 1881, independent of the Charter. Under Act XIII. of 1875, probate or letters granted by a High Court have effect throughout the whole of British India. Under Act VI. of 1881 the High Court may appoint District Delegates to grant probate and letters in non-contentious cases.

Matrimonial.

It also is vested with jurisdiction in matters matrimonial between Her Majesty's subjects professing the Christian religion.*

Its insolvency, maritime, and divorce jurisdiction will be described at the end of this lecture.

Madras and Bombay High Courts.

The first Charters of the Madras and Bombay High Courts bear date the 26th of June, 1862. They were subsequently superseded by a further Charter of the same date as that which applies to Calcutta. They are similar in all respects to the Calcutta Charter, *mutatis mutandis.* The local limits of the ordinary civil original jurisdiction of either Court are such as may be fixed by a law of the Governor in Council, and until so fixed were the limits of the jurisdiction of the Supreme Court at the date of its abolition. The criminal jurisdiction extends over the limits just described and also over all persons beyond those limits who were subject to the criminal jurisdiction of the Supreme Court.

North-West Provinces.

In March, 1866, Letters Patent were issued establishing a High Court in the North-Western Provinces of the Bengal Presidency.

Result of the establishment of High Courts.

The result of the establishment of the High Courts was to combine the Judges of the Supreme and Sudder Courts, and thereby to constitute a single tribunal. But as far as the policy

* The date of the first Charter of the Bengal High Court is 14th May, 1862; and of the second, 28th December, 1865.

LECTURE X.

of fusing two rival systems of judicial administration was concerned, no great advance was thereby made. The Supreme Court in reality survived as a distinct branch of the High Court, *viz.*, in its original side. The local extent of its jurisdiction, however, was confined within the limits of Calcutta; neither the agreement of parties nor the national character of individuals being any longer sufficient to give the Court a power of adjudication. The law or equity which it enforces on its original side is the same as would have been applied by the old Supreme Court, and is distinct from the rules of law, equity, and good conscience applied by the appellate side which succeeds to the old Sudder Court. The criminal and admiralty, testamentary, and matrimonial jurisdictions of the High Court in its original side were precisely the same as those exercised by the tribunal to which it succeeded. Its criminal procedure, too, remained distinct from that of the appellate side. The real innovation was that the civil procedure of the old Supreme Court was swept away, and Act VIII. of 1859 was substituted as the Code uniformly and universally applicable throughout India. Progressive legislation, establishing as time went on a body of Anglo-Indian law applicable in both Courts, has eventually completed, or nearly so, the fusion which was originally contemplated.

Uniformity, however, in the criminal law (the Penal Code having come into force on 1st January, 1862) and in the civil procedure of all Courts, and in civil and criminal appellate authority, dates from 1862.

The establishment of these High Courts and the passing of the Indian Councils' Act, 1861, seem to have led to a general reconstitution of Courts of Judicature throughout the country both in the regulation and in the non-regulation Provinces. In the Punjab, a Chief Court has been established, which is framed very much upon the model of the High Courts. It derives its existence from an Act of the Imperial Legislative Council, instead of a Royal Charter, and the Judges who compose it are appointed by the Governor-General in Council, and not by Her Majesty. It came into existence about the same time that the High Court of the North-West Provinces was established by Royal Charter.

Punjab chief Court.

It was established by Act IV. of 1866, passed with the previous sanction of the Secretary of State for India in Council, to amend the constitution of the Judicial Commissioner's Court. Act XVII. of 1877, and later on, Act XVIII. of 1884, c. 2, reconstituted it. This Act is amended by Act XIX. of 1895, and Act XXV. of 1899. The new tribunal was invested with an original jurisdiction for the trial of certain civil and criminal cases. It consists of three or more Judges. They hold their offices at the pleasure of the Governor-General. The Chief Court is the highest Court of Appeal from the Civil and Criminal Courts in the Punjab; over which it has a general supervision and control. Its proceedings are regulated by the civil procedure for the time being in force in the Punjab; and in exercising its jurisdiction it is bound to apply the rules of law or equity and good conscience which the local Court would have applied. It has complete jurisdiction over European British subjects, and it has superintendence over all Courts subject to its appellate jurisdiction.

Thus four High Courts were established for the three Presidencies, and a Chief Court for the Province of the Punjab—possessing the highest civil and criminal jurisdiction in the territories for which they were respectively established.

Retention of the old Presidency Town system.

Very little in reality was thereby effected towards amalgamating the Presidency Town and Mofussil systems of judicial organization. But subsequent legislation in this country reconstituted almost all the Civil and Criminal Courts of the country. I shall refer to it hereafter. At present I will pass on to institutions which chiefly belong to what I have

LECTURE X.

described as the Presidency Town system, and describe them in detail.

Insolvency Courts.

With regard to the establishment of Courts for the relief of insolvent debtors in British India, they were first established by Act of Parliament in 1829.* They were directed to be holden from the 1st of March, 1829, once a month at least throughout the year, and oftener, if need be, in Calcutta, and as often as found necessary within the towns of Madras and Bombay, by any one Judge of the Supreme Court of the Presidency. Though presided over by a Judge of the Supreme Court, the Insolvency Court had a distinct and separate existence. An appeal lay from it under the statute to the Supreme Court, which had power to make rules to facilitate the relief of insolvent debtors in cases for which sufficient provision had not been made in the Act. Four years was the period assigned as the duration of the Act, which was afterwards extended by subsequent enactments to the year 1848, when the Act was repealed; the Insolvent Courts, however, being at the same time re-established.

Previous to the establishment of those Courts by the Act of 1829, an Act of Parliament† passed in the year 1800 was the basis of jurisdiction to grant relief to insolvent debtors in India. It empowered the Supreme Courts at Fort William and Madras and the Recorder's Court at Bombay to make rules and orders, extending to insolvent debtors in India the relief intended by an Act of Parliament called the Lords' Act, passed in 1759. It ratified all rules and orders previously made by the Supreme Courts for granting such relief, and confirmed the acts done under such rules and orders.

In 1848,‡ an Act of Parliament was passed to consolidate and amend the law relating to insolvent debtors in India. It provided that the Courts of 1829 should be continued. Their §

* 9 Geo. IV. c. 73.

† 39 & 40 Geo. III. c. 79.

‡ 11 Vict. c. 21.

§ *Ibid.*, sec. 5.

jurisdictions severally extend to the disposal of all petitions by persons imprisoned within the limits of the Presidency Towns upon any process whatever, or who shall reside within the jurisdiction of any of the Supreme Courts and be in insolvent circumstances.

Insolvency jurisdiction in the Mofussil.

As regards the Mofussil in general there was no law of insolvency and no Courts for the relief of insolvent debtors. The Civil Courts could, however, under the operation of Section 271* of Act VIII. of 1859, effect some of the purposes of insolvency law, subject however to this, that the creditor who first attached the property of the debtor was entitled to be paid in full while the rest of the creditors were paid rateably. Such a provision led to a scramble amongst creditors, in which an unfortunate debtor or his property stood little chance of quarter or of consideration, while the successful creditor himself could not justify his priority on any principle of equity or fairness. Some provisions with respect to insolvency were to be found in what was called the Civil Code of the Punjab, and also in Major Spark's Code, applicable to parts of British Burma.

The insolvency law which is at present administered in India is as follows. The Court for the relief of insolvent debtors at a Presidency Town is held before one of the Judges of the High Court in accordance with the Charter of the High Court; and the provisions of 11 & 12 Vict. c. 21, continue to be applied therein. The jurisdiction of each extends over

* The Section was as follows:—

"If, after the claim of the person on whose application the property was attached has been satisfied in full from the proceeds of the sale, any surplus remain, such surplus shall be distributed rateably amongst any other persons who, prior to the order for such distribution, may have taken out execution of decrees against the same defendant, and not obtained satisfaction thereof. Provided that when any property is sold subject to a mortgage, the mortgagee shall not be entitled to share in any surplus arising from such sale."

Lecture X.

two classes of persons—those who are imprisoned in the Presidency Town and those who reside within the jurisdiction of the old Supreme Court of the Presidency. Each High Court, therefore, succeeded to the powers of the Supreme Court, which it displaced. As regards Bengal, however, the 17th clause of the Charter of 1862, which gave insolvent jurisdiction *within or without* the Bengal division of the Presidency, was replaced by clause 18 of the Charter of 1865, narrowing the jurisdiction to the Bengal division only, that is to that portion of it which is ruled by the Lieutenant-Governor of Bengal.* Apparently that restriction was with a view to conferring insolvency jurisdiction on the High Court for the North-West; but the Charter of 1866 constituting that Court is silent on the point. Then with regard to the Mofussil, Chap. XX. of Act X. of 1877, and afterwards of Act XIV. of 1882, confers insolvency jurisdiction on the District Courts generally. There is, therefore, a complete insolvency law for India, wherein the Civil Procedure Code applies; but it is not to interfere with the administration of the Act of Parliament, 11 & 12 Vict. c. 21, by those Courts which are empowered to administer it.

Vice-Admiralty Courts.

With regard to Vice-Admiralty Courts, the Crown was empowered in 1800† to issue a Commission from the High Court of Admiralty in England for the trial and adjudication of prize causes and all other maritime questions arising in India, and to nominate all or any of the Judges at the respective Presidency Towns, either alone or jointly with others, to be the Commissioners for carrying out the purposes of the Commission. In William the Fourth's reign an Act‡ was passed which gave an appeal to the High Court of Admiralty in certain cases. It defined the jurisdiction of the Vice-Admiralty Court to extend to all cases where a ship or

* See *In re* Tietkins, 1 B. L. R. O. C. J. 84.

† 39 & 40 Geo. III. c. 79, s. 25.

‡ 2 Will. IV. c. 51.

vessel or the master thereof should come within the local limits of any Vice-Admiralty Court; irrespective of the cause of action having arisen out of those limits.

A separate Vice-Admiralty Court appears to have been established in Calcutta in 1822. The Charters of the High Courts in 1862 and 1865 conferred the same civil and maritime jurisdiction on the Vice-Admiralty Court, and the same jurisdiction for the trial and adjudication of prize causes and other maritime questions arising in India, as was vested in Commissioners under the Act of George III.*

Divorce Courts.

In 1869 the High Courts were constituted by Act IV. of 1869, passed by the Governor-General in Council, Courts of Divorce of persons professing the Christian religion. The Chief Court of the Punjab first of the tribunals not established by Royal Charter was vested with a similar jurisdiction, *viz.* the power of granting, upon grounds which would entitle to a divorce in England, a final decree for dissolution of marriage. British Burma in that respect is placed within the jurisdiction of the High Court of Bengal; and all other non-regulation Provinces, and places in the dominions of allied Princes and States, are placed in respect of Christian subjects of Her Majesty residing therein under the jurisdiction of the particular High or Chief Court within whose original criminal jurisdiction the petitioner for divorce would have been subject, if a European British subject. The District Courts, both in regulation and non-regulation Provinces, have also a concurrent divorce jurisdiction with the High or Chief Courts to whose appellate jurisdiction they are subject, but it does not extend to the making a final decree for dissolution. Later Acts have extended divorce jurisdiction: see Act XXI. of 1866 in regard to native converts to Christianity, Act XV. of 1875 in regard to Parsis and Madras, Act IV. of 1896 in regard to certain Malabar Hindus.

* 39 & 40 Geo. III. c. 79. See the Colonial Courts of Admiralty (India), Act XVI. of 1891.

LECTURE XI.

THE INFERIOR CIVIL COURTS.

Courts of British Burma—Recorders' Courts—Existing Courts in Burma —Upper Burma — Lower Burma — Non-Regulation Territories—Central Provinces — Punjab — Oudh — Sind, Aden and Coorg—Appellate Procedure in these Courts—Civil Courts in Bombay—Civil Courts in Bengal and N.W.P. and Assam—Powers of High Court over the Civil Courts—Of the District Judge—Madras—General observations—Small Cause Courts—Act IX. of 1850—Act XXVI. of 1864—Act XV. of 1882—Mofussil Small Cause Courts.

As soon as the Legislature was reconstituted under the Indian Councils' Act, and was vested with a complete power of legislation over the non-regulation Provinces, it began to provide a system of Courts whose powers and jurisdiction should be based upon its own enactments.

Courts of British Burma.

The first country which attracted the attention of the Legislature was British Burma, and by Act I. of 1863 six grades of Courts were established in addition to Recorders' and Small Cause Courts thereafter to be established; the Chief Commissioner's being the highest. The Act maintained all the existing classes of Courts in British Burma, defined the jurisdiction to be exercised by each grade of those Courts, and laid down rules for the admission of regular as well as special and second appeals. It extended to British Burma generally the Code of Civil Procedure which had already been in force under an order of the Supreme Government in the entire territory except the Province of Pegu. It also extended to Pegu the Limitation Act XIV. of 1859.

Recorders' Courts.

Then came Act XXI. of 1863, which was passed apparently with the object of reviving on new soil the old Recorders' Courts, which had once flourished in Calcutta, Madras, and Bombay. Under it there was established at Rangoon and Moulmein a Court presided over by a barrister or advocate of five years' standing appointed by the Governor-General in Council, with full powers of civil and criminal jurisdiction. An appeal lay to Her Majesty in Council from the Recorder in all cases of the value of Rs. 10,000 or upwards, and to the High Court of Bengal in all cases between the value of 3000 and 10,000 rupees. The Recorder moreover was vested with all the powers of a Court of Session as defined in the Code of Criminal Procedure within certain territorial limits, except that he had no power to try, but only to commit to the Bengal High Court, any European British subject charged with an offence punishable with death.

Existing Courts in Burma.

Act VII. of 1872 repealed both these Acts and for three years regulated the Courts in British Burma. The Chief Commissioner had found that his executive duties prevented him from properly discharging the judicial business thrown upon him. The principal object of the new Act was to relieve him of that burden. A Judicial Commissioner was constituted thereby to the head of the Judicial system of the Province, and to have most of the powers of a High Court. The Recordership of Moulmein was discontinued.

Then came Act XVII. of 1875, which repealed Act VII. of 1872, and * till 1889 regulated the Courts of British Burma. Six grades of Civil Courts were established, the two lowest Courts being held by extra Assistant Commissioners. Above them in order were the Court of the Deputy Commissioner, of the Judge of the town of Moulmein, of the Commissioner, and highest of all of the Judicial Commissioner. The Court

* It was amended in 1884 and 1885.

LECTURE XI.

of the Recorder was continued; with a jurisdiction similar to that conferred upon him originally by Act XXI. of 1863. It included divorce, insolvency and admiralty jurisdiction.

Upper Burma.

In 1886 the territories of King Thebaw became part of British India and are known as Upper Burma, the former dominion of the Queen being entitled Lower Burma. By Regulations VII. and VIII. of 1886, passed under 33 Vict. c. 3,* and later on by Regulations I. and VI. of 1896, criminal and civil courts were established therein similar to those established in other parts of India; the law in force being declared by Upper Burma Laws Act XX. of 1886, and its amendments.

Lower Burma.

In Lower Burma Act XI. of 1889 repealed Act XVII. of 1875 and until 1900 established the Courts of that country. The six grades of civil courts were retained under the superintendence of the Judicial Commissioner. So also the Court of the Recorder of Rangoon, with his former jurisdiction, who held his court ordinarily at Rangoon, but might be directed by the local government to hold it on any particular occasion anywhere in Lower Burma in a civil case, and anywhere in Lower or Upper Burma in a criminal case in which a European British subject is concerned. In such criminal cases the Recorder was made the High Court for the whole of Burma. A special Court was continued by this Act composed ordinarily of the Judicial Commissioner and Recorder sitting together, though the local government might add thereto the judge of Moulmein; with a defined appellate jurisdiction, and with the powers of a High Court in certain criminal matters.

Then came Act VI. of 1900, which for the first time established a Chief Court composed of a Chief Judge and three or more other judges, as the highest Civil and Criminal Court of Appeal for the whole of Lower Burma, and as the High Court for the whole of the territories administered by

* See *ante*, p. 87.

the Lieut.-Governor of Lower Burma, including the Shan States in reference to proceedings against European British subjects. The Chief Court is also the principal Civil and Criminal Court of original jurisdiction for the Rangoon Town exerciseable by a single judge; with appeal to a bench thereof consisting of two other judges. It is vested with a general superintendence and control over all other Civil Courts in Lower Burma. Four grades of Civil Courts were established: (1) the Township Court; (2) the Sub-divisional Court; (3) the District Court; (4) the Divisional Court, with a power of appeal from a lower to a higher Court. The effect of this Act is that the appellate jurisdiction of the High Court of Bengal in cases between Rs. 3000 and Rs. 10,000, which had lasted for 37 years, was abolished. The Court known as the Special Court, which had been continued by Act XI. of 1889, composed of the Judicial Commissioner and Recorder of Rangoon, was also abolished.

Non-regulation territories.

Then, with regard to the non-regulation Provinces of Oudh, the Central Provinces, the Punjab, and other territories, no attempt had been made to provide distinct and matured systems of judicial administration, such as had been conferred on the three Presidencies. The systems which existed had been hurriedly framed as the territories to which they related were from time to time annexed. The legislation relating to these and other matters was to be found in numerous rules and orders which acquired the force of law under Section 25 of the Indian Councils' Act. The Legislature accordingly proceeded to establish Courts and define judicial authority in those Provinces by its own enactments.

Central Provinces.

In the Central Provinces there were eight grades of Courts established by Act XIV. of 1865, in addition to Courts of Small Causes and to any other Courts thereafter to be established. Act. XVI. of 1885 has reconstituted them; being

LECTURE XI.

itself amended by Act IV. of 1901. The highest Court is that of the Judicial Commissioner. It is declared by the Act to be the highest Civil Court of Appeal. The lowest Court is that of the tehsildar of the second class, with jurisdiction in suits of every description up to Rs. 100 in value; next to him the tehsildar of the first class, with jurisdiction up to Rs. 300; next to him the Assistant Commissioners of the third class, the second class and the first class, with jurisdiction up to Rs. 500, Rs. 1000, and Rs. 5000 respectively; sixthly, the Deputy Commissioner, whose original jurisdiction is not limited to any pecuniary amount, and who has power to hear appeals from decisions and orders of Courts subordinate to him; and seventhly, the Commissioner whose jurisdiction is without pecuniary limit and who exercises appellate jurisdiction over his assistants and deputies, being in turn subject to the appellate jurisdiction of the Judicial Commissioner.

Punjab. By Act XIX. of 1865 seven similar grades of Courts were established in the Punjab, *viz.*, a Court of the tehsildar, of three Assistant Commissioners with ordinary special and full powers, a Deputy Commissioner, a Commissioner, and a Judicial Commissioner. And by Act IV. of 1866, in lieu of the Court of the Judicial Commissioner, there was constituted the Chief Court of the Punjab (which is a High Court within the meaning of the Civil Procedure Code), consisting of Judges appointed by the Governor-General in Council. Then Act XVII. of 1877 was passed combining all the Courts under one Act. At present they are regulated by Act XVIII. of 1884, amended by Act XIII. of 1888, and Act XXV. of 1899, and consist of a Chief Court and four subordinate Courts, *viz.*, the Divisional, the District, the Court of the Subordinate Judge, and the Court of the Moonsiff.

Oudh. The Oudh grades of Courts were established by Act XIV. of 1865, similar to those provided for the Central Provinces.

That Act, however, was framed chiefly with reference to the Central Provinces; it was found incomplete as regards Oudh, and inconvenient, having regard to some subsequent legislation in reference to that territory. Accordingly, in 1871, the Oudh Civil Courts' Act * was passed, which applies to all Civil Courts in Oudh. It constitutes five grades of Courts, *viz.* those of (1) the Tehsildar; (2) the Assistant or Extra-Assistant Commissioner; (3) the Deputy Commissioner or the Civil Judge of Lucknow; (4) the Commissioner; (5) the Judicial Commissioner. Later on, Act XIII. of 1879 repealed this enactment, and provided that there should be four grades of Civil Courts in Oudh, *viz.*:—(1) the Munsif; (2) the Subordinate Judge; (5) the District Judge; (4) the Judicial Commissioner. They are all appointed, and the limits of their jurisdiction fixed, by the Local Government, the previous sanction of the Governor-General in Council being necessary in the case of the Judicial Commissioner. The general control over all the Courts in any district is vested in the District Judge, subject to the general control of the Judicial Commissioner. The Court of the District Judge is the principal Civil Court of original jurisdiction in his district. He entertains appeals from the Courts of the first two grades, and his own decisions may be appealed to the Judicial Commissioner. Act XIV. of 1891 and Act XVI. of 1897 provide for the appointment of additional Judicial Commissioners in some cases to exercise the jurisdiction of the Judicial Commissioner, in other cases to sit with him and form a Special Court.

LECTURE XI.

Sind, Aden and Coorg.

Courts were also established in Sind by Act XII. of 1866 (Bombay Code), at Aden by Act II. of 1864, and in Coorg by Regulation II. of 1881, which was passed by the Governor-General in pursuance of the legislative power conferred on him by 33 Vict. c. 3.

* Act XXXII. of 1871.

LECTURE XI.

Appellate procedure in these Courts.

The systems * thus established in the non-regulation Provinces differ chiefly with regard to the procedure adopted in the matter of appeal. In some cases a second appeal on the merits was given, which was in some Provinces final, in others liable to a further special appeal. In other cases no right of second appeal was given, but an extraordinary power of revision was vested in the Appellate Courts. The principle which eventually found most favour with the Legislature, to judge from the discussion upon the Oudh Bill, was to grant a second appeal on the merits when the Court of first appeal differed from the Court of first instance. In the case of Oudh the further provision was made in 1871 that such second appeal should in all cases lie to the highest Court of appeal in the Province.

Civil Courts in Bombay.

Next with regard to Courts subordinate to those established by Royal Charters granted in pursuance of the Imperial Act of 1861, Act XIV. of 1869 was passed in reference to the Presidency of Bombay. The law which regulated the constitution of the Civil Courts in that Presidency was considered to be in an unsatisfactory state. It was contained in unrepealed fragments of regulations passed in the years 1827, 1830, 1831, 1833, and 1834, which enacted such modifications of the original system as experience suggested; and thus,† although the law when ascertained was simple enough, it came to be stated in so complicated a way that there were few persons by whom it was thoroughly understood. The new Act (amended by Act IX. of 1880 and some later Acts) reproduced the essential provisions of those Regulations, and effected several amendments and alterations.

It appears that the law ‡ relating to Principal Sudder Ameens and Moonsiffs in Bengal had been previously

* Legislative Proceedings, India, Vol. X., 1871, p. 595.

† Legislative Proceedings, India, Vol. VIII., p. 11.

‡ Act XVI. of 1868.

consolidated. The object of the Bombay Act was to effect a similar work of consolidation. In lieu of three grades of Subordinate Civil Judges, *viz.*, Principal Sudder Ameens, Sudder Ameens and Moonsiffs, two grades of Subordinate Judges were established, *viz.*, of the first class with jurisdiction up to Rs. 10,000, and second class with jurisdiction up to Rs. 5000. The District Judge was enabled to hold his Court at any town in his district. The Subordinate Judges were empowered to hold their Courts in more places than one within the local limits of their jurisdiction.

The Act extends to the territories under the Governor of Bombay in Council other than Sind in which the Code of Civil Procedure was on the day of the passing of the Act in force; and may be extended by the local Government, which is empowered to fix the limits of districts and to appoint District Judges. The local Government may also with the sanction of the Governor-General in Council appoint in any district a joint Judge with the powers of a District Judge and a jurisdiction concurrent with his; also Assistant Judges, to whom the District Judge may refer original suits up to Rs. 10,000 in amount, but not appeals; also the Subordinate Judges before mentioned of two classes.

Thus, as regards the Bombay Presidency, the Punjab, the Central Provinces, British Burma, and other non-regulation territories, the entire law by which the system of judicial administration is regulated is set forth in the several Courts Acts relating to those territories; but down to 1871, in order to ascertain in Bengal, and down to 1873, in order to ascertain in Madras, the exact constitution and jurisdiction of the Civil Courts, it was necessary, as I have previously shown, to institute a laborious search through the regulations.

Civil Courts in Bengal

In 1871 it was found expedient to consolidate and amend the law relating to the District and Subordinate Civil Courts

LECTURE XI.

and N.W.P. and Assam.

in the Lower and North-Western Provinces of the Presidency of Bengal. Accordingly Act VI. of that year * was passed by the Governor-General in Council, called the Bengal Civil Courts Act, 1871. Act XII. of 1887 was subsequently passed, consolidating the law relating to those Courts and to the Courts of Assam. It is under this later Act † that the Judges of those Courts, of which there are four classes now, exercise their jurisdiction. It gives to the Government power to fix from time to time the number of District Judges and of the Subordinate Judges and Moonsiffs in each district; and on the recommendation of the High Court, subject to the sanction of the Governor-General in Council, to appoint Additional Judges.

It gives to the District Judge, subject to the superintendence of the High Court, the general control over all the Courts in his district. The local Government is vested with power to fix and alter the local limits of the jurisdiction of any Civil Court under the Act. The Judge or Subordinate Judge has cognizance of all original suits subject to the provisions of the Civil Procedure Code; but the Moonsiff's jurisdiction is limited to suits not exceeding Rs. 1000, though by notification the local Government may extend it to Rs. 2000. The District Judge has an appellate jurisdiction in reference to the decrees and orders of Subordinate Judges and Moonsiffs except where the amount or value of the subject-matter in dispute exceeds Rs. 5000, in which case the appeal lies to the High Court. The High Court also entertains appeals from decrees and orders of District and Additional Judges. The District Judge has power to refer to any Subordinate Judge under his control and subsequently to withdraw from him any appeals pending from the decisions of Moonsiffs.

* See ante, p. 123.

† See, however, Acts VII. of 1889, VIII. and XX. of 1890.

The local Government has power to suspend and remove for misconduct any District, Additional or Subordinate Judge or Moonsiff.

Powers of High Court over the Civil Courts.

The powers of the High Court, in regard to these judicial officers are (1) that in case of urgent necessity it may suspend a Subordinate Judge and forthwith report to the local Government the circumstances of the suspension, the final order in the matter resting with the local Government; (2) it may appoint a Commission for inquiring into the alleged misconduct of any Moonsiff, and according to the result of such inquiry, remove or suspend him; (3) it may suspend him pending the result of the inquiry, or it may proceed to punishment without appointing any Commission.

Of the District Judge.

A District Judge also may, in case of urgent necessity, suspend a Moonsiff and report the circumstance to the High Court, with whom the power of making a final order rests.

Madras.

In reference to Madras, Act III. of 1873 * contains provisions for the Courts of the districts of that Presidency similar to those which are contained in Act VI. of 1871; except that the Moonsiff has jurisdiction up to Rs. 2500. The Act extends to the whole Presidency, exclusive of those tracts which are subject to the agents for Ganjam and Vizagapatam. Act VII. of 1892 established an additional Civil Court for the city.

General observations.

Such is a short sketch of the existing judicial institutions of India. They are nearly all of them of recent origin, dating their establishment from enactments and Charters which have all been passed since 1861. Acts of the Legislative Council, apart from the old regulations, have become the foundation of all the Courts in India, except those expressly constituted by Royal Charter. The whole of them might probably be consolidated in one Civil Courts Code, establishing throughout the country in every province a gradation

* Amended by Act XXI. of 1885.

LECTURE XI.

of Courts similar in title and jurisdiction. At the present time, however, there is a wide difference between the regulation and the non-regulation of Provinces in respect of this, that in the latter the officers who hold the different Courts which I have described have executive as well as judicial functions. They divide amongst them almost the whole executive work of their respective provinces. The Judges of the Chief Court in the Punjab and those of the Small Cause Courts are the only Judges in that province who perform exclusively judicial functions. The same plan is observed in Oudh and the Central Provinces, and was till very recently in British Burmah. In the two first there is a Court of a Judicial Commissioner instead of a Chief Court. In the latter there was a Chief Commissioner, who was also head of the Executive, but under Act VII. of 1872 a Judicial Commissioner was first appointed, whose functions remain purely judicial.

The mode in which these Courts are * placed in regular degrees of subordination is exhibited by the general law of appeals, which so far as the chief appellate authority is concerned, depend upon the High Courts' Charters and the Civil Procedure Code. An appeal to the High Court must be determined by a Bench of two or more Judges. If they (*i.e.*, the two) differ, the opinion of the senior Judge prevails, and another appeal is given to a Bench of three Judges. The Appellate Court can remand the case for further trial, or it can itself take further evidence.

The actual course of appeal differs in the different provinces. There are in Bengal, Madras, and the North-Western Provinces four kinds of Judges—Moonsiffs, Subordinate Judges, District Judges, and High Court Judges; Sudder Ameens and Principal Sudder Ameens having been

* Mr. Fitz-James Stephen's Minute on the Administration of Justice in India.

abolished, Moonsiffs may try cases up to Rs. 1000 or Rs. 2000 (in Madras up to Rs. 2500), and an appeal lies from their decision to the District Judge.

From the decisions of Subordinate Judges the appeal lies to the District Judge if the value of the case does not exceed Rs. 5000, and in all other cases direct to the High Court. The original jurisdiction, on the other hand, of the District Judges is unlimited in amount, including an important miscellaneous civil jurisdiction, as for instance, under the Succession Act, the Divorce Act, and the like. The appeal from their decisions lies to the High Court.

In Bombay, Moonsiffs, as well as Ameens, are abolished, and there are five kinds of Judges, *viz.*, Subordinate Judges of two classes; (1) those who may try cases up to Rs. 5000; (2) those who may try cases beyond that amount; above them District Judges, with their Assistant Judges under them, and their Joint Judges, with concurrent jurisdiction; and finally High Court Judges.

District Judges are the principal Courts of original civil jurisdiction in the district, and are also Courts of Appeal from all decrees and orders passed by subordinate Courts, except from decrees above Rs. 5000, in which case the appeal lies to the High Court. There are also Joint Judges and Judges having concurrent jurisdiction with District Judges, but doing such civil business only as they receive from the District Judge or the High Courts.

Assistant Judges are subordinate to the District Judges, and may try any cases referred to them by the District Judges not exceeding Rs. 10,000, and not being in the nature of appeals. An appeal lies from such Assistant, as from a subordinate first class, to the District Judge in cases under Rs. 5000, and in cases exceeding that amount to the High Court.

Small Cause Courts.

Besides the judicial organization which I have just

LECTURE XI. described, the courts of the country include a variety of tribunals established for the purpose of adjudicating upon small causes in a less expensive and more expeditious manner than is possible in those which have been described in this and in the last lecture. A sketch of these will conclude the account of the existing Civil Courts of British India.

The Courts of Small Causes in the Presidency Towns, as they now exist, were originally established under Act IX. of 1850. They are the successors of the old Courts of Requests, which were established at Calcutta, Madras, and Bombay in 1753, by the Charter of George II.; the limit of their jurisdiction being originally five pagodas, subsequently in 1797,* extended to Rs. 80. Two years later, an Act † of Parliament was passed to enable the Governors of Calcutta and Madras to extend the jurisdiction of those Courts to Rs. 400 sicca, to alter and reform the constitution and practice of the Courts, and to frame new rules and orders. By proclamation, in pursuance of this Act, Commissioners were appointed for the recovery of small debts in Bengal, and the jurisdiction of the Court was extended in 1819 to Rs. 400 sicca. The Courts of Requests at all the Presidencies were, by the Charter of Justice and by the proclamations, placed under the control of the Supreme Court, in the same manner that inferior Courts in England were placed under the control of the Court of Queen's Bench, and they continued to exist till 1850.

Act IX. of 1850. In that year an Act was passed repealing the provisions of George II.'s Charter, and all Acts made concerning the constitution or practice of the Courts of Requests. Courts of Small Causes were established as Courts of Record, with jurisdiction conterminous with that of the abolished Courts;

* 37 Geo. III. c. 142, s. 30.

† 39 & 40 Geo. III. c. 79, s. 17.

the judges were to be appointed by the Governor in Council, and to have cognizance over all suits when the debt or damage claimed or the value of the property in dispute was not more than Rs. 500, whether on balance of account or otherwise. It was provided that any Judge or Judges of the Supreme Court who should consent to aid in the execution of the Act, might exercise all the powers of a Judge appointed under it, and might try suits as if he were a Small Cause Court Judge. All suits brought in the Small Cause Court were directed to be heard and determined in a summary way, and every defence which would be deemed good in the Supreme Court, sitting as a Court of Equity, was declared to be a bar to any legal demand in the Court of Small Causes. LECTURE XI.

In 1864 an Act* was passed extending the jurisdiction of these Courts to the recovery of any debt, damage, or demand, exceeding the sum of Rs. 500, but not exceeding the sum of Rs. 1000, provided that the cause of action should have arisen, or the defendant, at the time of bringing the action, should dwell or carry on business, or personally work for gain, within the local limits of the jurisdiction of the Court. Moreover, by consent of parties the Court had jurisdiction in cases exceeding in value the sum of Rs. 1000. In cases exceeding Rs. 500 in value, the judges were directed to reserve doubtful questions of law or equity for the opinion of the High Court, and to give judgment contingent upon that opinion. Act XXVI. of 1864.

Act XV. of 1882 repealed all prior enactments, and at present constitutes the Small Cause Courts of the Presidency Towns. The law administered and the local limits of the jurisdiction correspond to the High Court in its ordinary original civil jurisdiction. With numerous exceptions specified in the Act they may try all civil suits when the amount or value of Act XV. of 1882.

* Act XXVI. of 1864.

LECTURE XI.

the subject-matter does not exceed Rs. 2000; the leave of the Court, however, being necessary in certain circumstances. The exceptions include, amongst others, cases concerning the revenue, acts ordered or done by the Executive or by officers, and immoveable property. They also include various suits belonging to equity, admiralty, and divorce jurisdiction. The Courts are subject to the superintendence of the High Courts. The Act has been amended by some later Acts.

Mofussil Small Cause Courts.

With regard to the Mofussil, Small Cause Courts were established * in 1860; and in 1865 the law relating to † them was consolidated and amended. Act IX. of 1887 reconstituted them. Suits to the value of Rs. 500, or, if the local Government so direct, to the value of Rs. 1000, are, generally speaking, cognizable by those Courts. There are, however, forty-four express exceptions; which are specified in the 2nd schedule to the Act of 1887.

The constitution of the Courts, with the establishment of officers, depends upon the local Government, the previous sanction of the Governor-General in Council being necessary. The territorial limits of each Court are defined, and may at any time be abolished by the local Government.

Power is no longer given to reserve questions for the opinion of the High Court, and to give judgment contingent thereon. But the High Court may for its own satisfaction call for a case decided by the Small Cause Court, and pass such order as it thinks fit.

* Act XLII. of 1860.
† Act XI. of 1865.

LECTURE XII.

THE INFERIOR CRIMINAL COURTS AND POLICE.

Introduction—Act X. of 1872—Three proposed alterations—Suggestions of the Local Government—Report of the Committee—Criminal liability of Europeans—The Criminal Courts established by the Code—Act X. of 1882 and Act V. of 1898—Distinction between the three classes of Magistrates—Magistrate of the District—Of the sub-division—Special Magistrates—Courts of Session—Powers of Criminal Courts over Europeans—Powers of the Magistrate—Powers of the Sessions Judge—Powers of High Courts—Police Administration generally—As Modified in Bengal—In Bombay Presidency—In Madras Presidency—In the Presidency Towns—Bombay—Calcutta—Suburbs of Calcutta—Madras—North-Western Provinces—Justices of the Peace—Coroners.

Introduction.

It remains to give an account of the Criminal Courts and Police organization now existing in British India. The system for the repression of crime is the most important branch of the Government of the country, the instrument by which peace and order, which are the chief objects of Government, are daily and in all the details of life secured..

Closely connected with this Judicial and Police organization is the subject of criminal procedure. The first Code on that subject was passed in 1861. It was the product of several generations of Indian administrators and statesmen, who from the first moment that they undertook the responsibility of Government, and abandoned a blind reliance on the Mahomedan Adawluts, had undertaken the task of framing by degrees a system on which criminal justice should proceed. The system which they originally established was

LECTURE XII. from time to time frequently altered, amended, and re-adjusted, and at length a hundred regulations and Acts were consolidated and compressed into a single Code.

Then came various amendments of the Code itself, and, in course of time, Act VIII. of 1869 consolidated these amendments.

Mr. Fitz-James Stephen * said of the Code of 1861 that it was "drawn by men thoroughly well acquainted with the system with which they were concerned; but I am inclined to doubt whether they did not know it rather too well, for they certainly threw the various provisions together with very little regard to arrangement and without any general plan." The result of the Amending Acts and of Act VIII. of 1869 was, he considered, only to increase the confusion which had previously existed.

Act X. of 1872.

The consequence was that the Criminal Procedure Code of 1872 was passed, which came into force on the 1st of September of that year. It repealed the Code of 1869 and so much of the Code of 1861 as had not been repealed, and various other Acts bearing upon minor points of criminal law and procedure. The later Code (*viz.*, Act VIII. of 1869) had made extensive amendments in the earlier law without repealing it, so that two Codes were in existence instead of one. The Act of 1872 entirely re-arranged the law, and also, which is the important point for our attention, reconstructed all the Criminal Courts throughout the Mofussil.

Three proposed alterations.

Three important alterations of law were proposed in reference to what I have described as the rival judicial institutions of the Crown and the Company. The object was to remove unnecessary distinctions, and establish greater uniformity of criminal jurisdiction and procedure.

The first related to the jurisdiction given by the Statute of

* Legislative Proceedings of the Council of India, Vol. XI., p. 392.

George III.*, to Justices of the Peace in the Mofussil, and exercised by them on European British subjects. It was proposed† that that jurisdiction should extend to cases usually disposed of before Magistrates upon summons.

The second alteration proposed was to enable Sessions Judges to dispose of all cases against European British subjects, unless they insisted upon their right to be tried by the High Courts.

The third was with regard to trial by juries. Instead of convicting a man if found guilty by a larger majority of a jury, and trying him again if found guilty by a smaller majority, the concurrence of the Judge was proposed to be the condition of the triumph of the majority. It was proposed therefore, that, if not less than two-thirds of a jury convicted, and the Judge agreed with them, the accused was to be convicted; if there was not such a majority, or if the Judge did not agree with them, the accused would be acquitted.

Suggestions of the Local Government.

While the Bill was pending before the Council the Government of Bengal suggested that, instead of the Justices of the Peace (who are generally Mofussil Magistrates) being limited in their penal powers over European British subjects to two months' imprisonment, as was the case under the Statute of George III., those powers should be considerably extended, and that European British subjects should be rendered amenable in a great degree to the ordinary Criminal Courts of the country. This suggestion was concurred in by other Local Governments, and the Select Committee appointed to consider the Bill reported—

Report of the Committee.

(1.) That a full power Magistrate, being a Justice of the Peace, and being, in the case of Mofussil Magistrates, a European British subject, should be empowered to try European British subjects for such offences as could be adequately

* 53 Geo. III. c. 155.

† See Legislative Proceedings (Indian Council), (1870), Vol. IX., p. 481.

punished by three months' imprisonment and a fine of Rs. 1000.

(2.) That a Sessions Judge, being a European British subject, should be empowered to pass a sentence on British subjects of one year, or fine; and that, if the European British subject pleads guilty, or accepts the Sessions Judge's jurisdiction, the Court may pass any sentence which is provided by law for the offence in question.

(3.) That a European British subject, convicted by a Justice of the Peace or Magistrate, should have a right of appeal, either to the Court of Session, or High Court, at his option.

(4.) That in every case in which a European is in custody, he may apply to a High Court for a writ of *habeas corpus*, and the High Court shall thereupon examine the legality of his confinement, and pass such order as it thinks fit.

This report shewed the general tendency of the new legislation, and challenged discussion upon the subject of the exclusive privileges of Europeans in criminal matters. It was important that the subject should be settled, and the extent of the privileges, which certainly rest upon a reasonable and fair foundation, ascertained. The further question relating to the extent to which uniform procedure in Presidency Town and Mofussil can be secured was left untouched.

Criminal liability of Europeans.

The system by which the exemption of Europeans from liability to the criminal jurisdiction of the Mofussil Courts was secured was considered to work a great and real political injury. It ensured to English wrong-doers practical immunity from punishment; the inconvenience and expense and difficulties attending their trial serving to render conviction uncertain and improbable. Two extreme opinions seemed to prevail upon this subject: one that to maintain any distinction at all between European and Native in respect of criminal offences was a great injustice, and contrary to the principles on which the British Government ought to rule; the other that Englishmen were entitled to trial by an English Jury, before an English Judge, in all cases of a degree above the class of petty offences with which a Justice of the Peace could deal in a summary manner. Mr. Fitz-James Stephen's views upon the matter were expressed in the following terms:—

"* In countries situated as most European countries are, it is no doubt desirable that there should be no personal law; but in India it is otherwise. Personal, as opposed to territorial laws, prevail here on all sorts of subjects, and their maintenance is claimed with the utmost pertinacity by those who are subject to them. The Mahomedan has his personal law. The Hindu has his personal law. Women, also, who according to the custom of the country ought not to appear in Court, are excused from appearing in Court. Natives of rank and influence enjoy, in many cases, privileges which stand on precisely the same principle; and are English people to be told that, whilst it is their duty to respect all those laws scrupulously, they are to claim nothing for themselves? that, whilst English Courts are to respect, and even to enforce a variety of laws which are thoroughly repugnant to all the strongest convictions of Englishmen, Englishmen who settle in this country are to surrender privileges to which, rightly or otherwise, they attach the highest possible importance? I can see no ground or reason for such a contention. I think there is no country in the world, and no race of men in the world, for whom a claim for absolute identity of law for all persons of all races and all habits comes with so bad a grace as from the natives of this country, filled as it is with every distinction which race, caste, and religion can create, and passionately tenacious as are its inhabitants of such distinctions."

* Legislative Proceedings of the Council of India, Vol. XI., p. 398.

LECTURE XII.

The Criminal Courts established by the Code.

Act X. of 1872 was a complete body of law upon three distinct subjects, *viz.*, the constitution of the Criminal Courts, the conduct of criminal proceedings, and the exercise of a preventive jurisdiction for the purpose of securing the peace.

It is only with the first of these subjects that we have to do. In that respect the Code proceeded upon the same principle as the Bengal Sessions Judges Act of 1871. It repealed a number of Acts and regulations which, in an obscure and fragmentary manner established Criminal Courts, and placed the constitution and powers of those Courts in a clear and distinct shape. The Chief Criminal Courts throughout the country have already been described. They include the High Courts, the Chief Court of the Punjab, the Court of the Recorder of Rangoon, and those highest Judicial Commissioners' Courts and Special Courts, which, in the non-regulation Provinces, exercise power of criminal revision, or appeal in the last resort. The Code enacted that besides these tribunals, there should be four grades of Criminal Courts in British India, being those mentioned further on, exclusive of those of the Presidency Magistrates.

The Code was amended by several Acts (*viz.*, XI. of 1874, X. of 1875, and IV. of 1877), and eventually a new Code (Act X. of 1882) was passed to consolidate and amend the law relating to criminal procedure. That Code applied to the whole of India, while Act X. of 1872 excluded from its operation High Courts in their original criminal jurisdiction and the Courts of Police Magistrates in the Presidency Towns. The new Code repealed, wholly or partially, a number of Acts, including Act X. of 1875, which regulated the criminal procedure of the High Courts, and Act IV. of 1877, which regulated that of the Presidency Magistrates.

Act X. of 1882 and Act V. of 1898.

Act X. of 1882 was subsequently replaced by Act V. of 1898. The later Act, like the former, enacted that besides High Courts, and Courts established under any other law than the Code, there should be five classes of Criminal Courts in British India, *viz.*:—

(1.) Courts of Session.

(2.) Presidency Magistrates.

(3.) Magistrates of the first class.

(4.) Magistrates of the second class.

(5.) Magistrates of the third class.

Distinction between the three classes of Magistrates.

All criminal trials in British India must be held before one or other of these Courts. The powers of a Court of Session extend to passing any sentence authorized by law; but any sentence of death passed by it is subject to confirmation by the High Court. An Assistant Sessions Judge may not exceed seven years' transportation or imprisonment. The main distinction between the other Courts is that a Presidency Magistrate and a Magistrate of the first class may sentence up to the term of two years, or impose a fine up to Rs. 1000; a Magistrate of the second class may imprison up to six months, or impose a fine up to Rs. 200; both of them may include in the imprisonment solitary confinement, and may, if in the case of a Magistrate of the second class he is specially authorized by the local Government, order a whipping. A Magistrate of the third class may imprison for one month, or impose a fine up to Rs. 50, but he may neither order solitary confinement, nor a whipping.

Any Magistrate may pass any lawful sentence combining any of the sentences which he is authorized by law to pass; that is to say he may award imprisonment in default of payment of a fine, in addition to the full term of imprisonment which he is competent to award.

Besides these three classes of Magistrates, the local Government must appoint in every district, outside the Presidency Towns, one of their number of the first class who shall be called the District Magistrate, and shall exercise throughout it all the powers of a Magistrate. It may also

LECTURE XII.

appoint subordinate Magistrates. In the non-regulation Provinces the local Government may invest the District Magistrate or any Magistrate of the first class with power to try as a Magistrate all offences not punishable with death.

Magistrate of the district.

All the Magistrates of the three classes shall be appointed by the Local Government, and shall be subordinate to the Magistrate of the district, the local limits of whose jurisdiction may be prescribed by the Local Government. All Magistrates are to be independent of the Sessions Judge, except to the extent and in the manner provided by the Code.

Of the sub-division.

The Local Government may divide districts outside the Presidency Towns into sub-divisions, and place any Magistrate of the first or second class in charge of a sub-division of a district. The Magistrate of the sub-division shall be subject to the control of the Magistrate of the district, but he in his turn shall control every Magistrate within his sub-division.

Special Magistrates.

Special Magistrates may be appointed by the Local Government in any local area outside the Presidency Towns. The Local Government may direct any two or more Magistrates to sit together as a Bench, and may invest such Bench with the powers of a Magistrate of the first, second, or third class, and direct the Bench so constituted to try such cases or such classes of cases only, and within such local limits as it thinks fit; and in the absence of such direction, the Bench shall have the powers of the highest class to which any one of its members who is present taking part in the proceedings belongs.

The Presidency Magistrates are appointed for the Presidency Towns, which for the purpose of the Code are to be deemed districts. One of such Magistrates in each town is to be Chief Magistrate.

Courts of Session.

With regard to Courts of Session, every province, excluding the Presidency Towns, shall be a sessions division (sec. 7), or shall consist of sessions divisions; and every division shall be a district or consist of districts; the Local Government being empowered to alter the number of such divisions and districts. There shall be a Court of Sessions and a Sessions Judge for every sessions division. The Local Government may appoint additional and Assistant Sessions Judges, who shall exercise all the powers of the Court, limited, however, as regards punishment, to seven years' transportation or imprisonment.

Any person (sec. 408) convicted on a trial held by an Assistant Sessions Judge, a District Magistrate, or other Magistrate of the first class, may appeal to the Court of Session. If such person is a European British subject he may at his option appeal either to the High Court or the Court of Session. Any one convicted by a Sessions Judge, or an Additional Sessions Judge, or by a Presidency Magistrate (if in this latter case he is sentenced to upwards of six months' imprisonment or Rs. 200 fine), may appeal to the High Court; except in cases where he has pleaded guilty, when there is no appeal except as to the extent or legality of the sentence. There is also an appeal to the High Court from any sentence of four years' imprisonment or transportation by an Additional Sessions Judge or by a Magistrate specially empowered. There is no appeal, however, in petty cases, that is, where the Court of Sessions or any Magistrate of the first class sentences to imprisonment not exceeding one month, or to a fine not exceeding Rs. 50, or to whipping only, nor is there any appeal from certain summary convictions.

Powers of Criminal Courts over Europeans.

The provisions of the Code, unless it is otherwise distinctly expressed, apply to all persons without distinction of race; but a separate chapter (c. 33) of it relates to the investigation and trial of offences committed by European British subjects.*

* These include (see interpretation clause of the Code) (1) all subjects of Her Majesty born, naturalized, or domiciled in the United Kingdom

LECTURE XII.

One provision in this exclusive chapter is that, in order to have any criminal jurisdiction in reference to a European British subject, the Judge of a Sessions Court must himself be of the same nationality; if an Assistant Sessions Judge he must also have held the office for at least three years and been especially empowered in that behalf by the Local Government. Another provision is that for purposes of investigation, the judicial officer must hold the double office of Magistrate of the first class, unless he is a District or Presidency Magistrate, and of Justice of the Peace, and must also be a European British subject.

Powers of the Magistrate.

Any Magistrate may entertain a complaint, and issue process to compel the appearance of the accused without regard to nationality; but if the accused is a European British subject, such process must be returnable before a Magistrate competent to inquire into or to try the case. Such Magistrate, being a Presidency Magistrate, shall have power to punish up to three months' imprisonment, or up to a fine of Rs. 1000, or both; being a District Magistrate, shall have power up to six months' imprisonment and Rs. 2000 fine, or both. In cases not adequately punished by a sentence of that character, the Magistrate must commit the accused to the Court of Session, unless the offence complained of be punishable with death or transportation for life, in which case the commitment shall be to the High Court. In the Presidency Towns the commitment is always to the High Court. In either Court he may claim to be tried before a mixed jury or a mixed set of assessors, not less than half being Europeans or Americans. He may also claim before a District Magistrate that his trial should be by jury.

of Great Britain and Ireland, or in any of the European, American or Australian colonies or possessions of Her Majesty, or in the colony of New Zealand, or in the colony of the Cape of Good Hope or Natal; (2) children and grandchildren of any such persons by legitimate descent.

Powers of the Sessions Judge.

Sessions Judges, or additional Sessions Judges, and, when specially empowered by the Local Government, Assistant Session Judges, who have held that rank for not less than three years, may pass on European British subjects any sentence warranted by law not exceeding one year's imprisonment, or fine, or both.

If, at any stage of the proceeding, the Sessions Judge thinks that such sentence would be inadequate, he shall record his opinion to that effect, and transfer the case to the High Court.

Powers of High Courts.

A European British subject, convicted by a Magistrate, or Assistant Sessions Judge, may, at his option, appeal to the Court of Session or to the High Court; convicted by a Court of Session he may appeal to the High Court. The High Court is vested with power to order any European who complains of unlawful detention within its jurisdiction to be brought before it to abide its further order.

The Magistrate is bound to ask any accused person, unless he has reason to believe that he is not a European British subject, whether he is or not; and if the accused does not claim before the Magistrate who tries or commits him to be dealt with as a European British subject, he shall be held to have waived his privilege.

Police administration generally.

With regard to the Police Administration in India, Act V. of 1861, modified by Act III. of 1888, and later on by Act VIII. of 1895, remains as the basis upon which the general law on that subject outside the Presidency Towns rests, modified in different localities by special Acts; which it is outside the scope of this work to discuss with any minuteness. It has been applied generally throughout the country.

As modified in Bengal.

In Bengal an Act was passed in 1867 which abolished Municipal Chokidars and provided (see, however, the Municipalities Act V. of 1876) that the Police in towns should be

Lecture XII.

enrolled under the general Act, the expenses to be provided by the town for which they were appointed. Act VII. of 1869 provided for the establishment of general Police Districts, each subject to an Inspector-General; while a system of village chowkeedars was established by Act VI. of 1870.

In Bombay Presidency.

In the Presidency of Bombay, excluding the town, a local Act was passed called the Bombay District Police Act, 1867. This was, however, repealed almost entirely by Bombay Act IV. of 1890, which provides that the superintendence of the Police throughout the Bombay Presidency shall vest in the Governor, and that its administration shall vest in an Inspector-General and his deputies; and in each district in a District Superintendent, subject to the control and direction of the Magistrate of the District. The duties and powers of the Police are provided for in the Act, *viz.*, Bombay Act IV. of 1890; amended by Act IV. of 1902. In exercising his authority the Magistrate of the District must be governed by the rules and orders of his Government. He may in case of pressing need call upon the Inspector-General to furnish him with additional police; and the District Superintendents are bound to furnish him with reports on any matters connected with crimes and the maintenance of order, and even to remove their subordinates on his requisition. The Commissioner in turn has certain powers within his division which are paramount to those of the Magistrate of the District.

In Madras Presidency

The Regulation of Police within the Madras territories is provided for by Act XXIV. of 1859, which was amended by a local Act, V. of 1865. The superintendence of the Police was vested in the Governor in Council, with power to give exclusive authority to others to appoint, supersede, or control any police functionary. An Inspector-General of Police with such subordinates as the Government may think fit are responsible for the administration of the force. Special

Police officers may be appointed in case of tumult or riot by the nearest Magistrate. The duties of Police officers are, to use their best endeavours and ability to prevent all crimes, offences, and public nuisances; to preserve the peace, to apprehend disorderly and suspicious characters, to detect and bring offenders to justice, to collect and communicate intelligence respecting the public peace, and promptly to obey and execute all orders and warrants lawfully issued to them.

In the Presidency Towns.

With regard to the three Presidency Towns, the Police administration was provided for by Acts XIII. of 1856 and XLVIII. of 1860, and those Acts, subject to frequent amendments, remained in force as far as the town of Bombay is concerned; until they were finally repealed by Bombay Act IV. of 1902, which consolidates the law relating to the police in that city.

Bombay.

Calcutta.

But in Calcutta, Act IV. of 1866 of the Bengal Council has repealed them so far as they relate to the town of Calcutta, and has provided that the administration of the Police in that town should be vested in an officer styled the Commissioner of Police and appointed by the Lieutenant-Governor, who can also appoint one or more deputies to perform any of the Commissioner's duties under his orders. A special Police Force is provided for the town of Calcutta, its strength being determined by the Lieutenant-Governor with the sanction of the Supreme Government. The Commissioner appoints them and may fine, suspend or dismiss them. He may appoint special constables, on emergency, with the powers of ordinary officers of Police.

Calcutta is divided into Police Districts by the Lieutenant-Governor, and the existing Magistrates of Police are appointed under this Act. The powers of the Magistrates, the Commissioner, and the Police are carefully defined under the Act.

Suburbs of Calcutta.

Ten days before this Act was passed another Act, *viz.*, II. of

Lecture XII.

1866 (Bengal Council), received the assent of the Governor-General. It enabled the Lieutenant-Governor to exclude the suburbs of the town of Calcutta from the general Police District of the Provinces, and to order the constitution of a Police Force therein to be under the exclusive direction and control of the Commissioner of Police for the town of Calcutta. No special Magistrate of Police is appointed for the suburbs, but the powers of the Commissioner therein are similar to those which he exercises in Calcutta. The municipal police continues to be regulated by local enactments.

Madras.

With regard to the town of Madras, the Police Acts XIII. of 1856 and XLVIII. of 1860 were repealed by the local Act VIII. of 1867, which in turn was repealed by Madras Act III. of 1888. The town Police was by the last Act constituted in such manner as the Governor in Council should direct. A Commissioner of Police was appointed for Madras, subject to the authority of the Governor in Council.

North-Western Provinces.

In 1869 an Act* was passed by the Governor-General in Council to provide for the maintenance of the rural Police in the North-Western Provinces and to define the law relating to village watchmen. Subsequently Act XVI. of 1873 repealed this Act, and provided for a village and road Police, omitting village watchmen. The village Police are to be appointed by the zemindars, the road Police by the Magistrate of the district. Their duties are prescribed by the Act. The Magistrate of the district may dismiss the members of either force. The Local Government may frame rules for their numbers, location, and discipline, and generally for the purposes of the Act.

Justice of the Peace.

In 1869 the law relating to the appointment of Justices of the Peace was consolidated and amended by Act II. of that year passed by the Governor-General of India in Council.

* Act III. of 1869.

The new Code of Criminal Procedure (V. of 1898), secs. 22 to 25, now contains the law on the subject. It is provided that outside the Presidency Towns the Governor-General of India in Council and every Local Government within its provinces may appoint such European British subjects as they may think fit to be Justices of the Peace within such territories as may be notified. For the three Presidency towns the appointment of Justices of the Peace rests generally with the Local Government. For those towns any persons resident within British India, and not being the subjects of any foreign State, who may be deemed qualified, are eligible. Outside the Presidency Towns existing Justices of the Peace are deemed to be appointed for the whole of India except the towns under the Act.

A Justice of the Peace may be suspended or dismissed by the Government which appointed him.

Coroners.

The law relating to Coroners in the Presidency Towns was consolidated by Act IV. of 1871. Every Coroner is appointed and may be suspended or removed by the Local Government. He must inquire into the cause of death whenever any person has died by accident, homicide, suicide, in prison, or suddenly by means unknown. On receiving notice of such death he must summon a jury, view and examine the body, summon witnesses, and finally draw up the inquisition according to the finding of the jury or the opinion of the majority. It is no longer the duty of the Coroner to inquire whether any person dying by his own Act was or was not *felo de se*, to inquire of treasure trove or wrecks, to seize any fugitive's goods, to execute process, or to exercise any Coroner's jurisdiction not especially conferred by this Act. The Act was subsequently amended by Act X. of 1881, and finally by the Criminal Procedure Codes (X. of 1882, and V. of 1898). Act V. of 1889 however abolished the office for Madras and made other provision for the discharge of its duties.

INDEX.

ACTS OF THE GOVERNOR-GENERAL IN COUNCIL—
continued.

THE END.

PRINTED BY WILLIAM CLOWES AND SONS, LIMITED, LONDON AND BECCLES.